AF541617

DYNAMICS OF RURAL POVERTY IN INDIA

DYNAMICS OF RURAL POVERTY IN INDIA

S. ERAPPA
INSTITUTE FOR SOCIAL AND ECONOMIC CHANGE
BANGALORE—560 072

DISCOVERY PUBLISHING HOUSE
NEW DELHI—110 002

Published by:
Namit Wasan
DISCOVERY PUBLISHING HOUSE PVT. LTD.
4383/4B, Ansari Road, Darya Ganj
New Delhi-110 002 (India)
Phone : +91-11-23279245; 23253475; 43596065
E-mail : discoverybooksindia@gmail.com
discoverypublishinghouse@gmail.com
namitwasan9@gmail.com
web : www.discoverypublishinggroup.com

Edition: **2020**

ISBN: 978-81-7141-312-6

Dynamics of Rural Poverty in India

Printed at:
Infinity Imaging Systems
Delhi

Preface

Irrespective of the development status of the country in the world, there exists the lower income strata, that is called as 'Core Poverty Group'. To alleviate this group for better living conditions, from time to time several strategies were devised, the most important of which is IRDP, initiated and implemented through state intervention in India. The main objective of all the poverty alleviation programmes is to make both i.e., beneficiaries and the programme sustainable to acheive the social justice, equity and development. Keeping this perspective in option, the empherical study conducted at ISEC has made an attempt to examine the conceptional issues on Poverty were classified into different schools of thought. And the theoritical issues were carefully looked since Merchantalist onwards. Further the role of state intervention and the financial institutions to assess the productivity of investment and witnessed changes occured at the rural poor households in Karnataka at two points of time. And the perceptions of the beneficiaries and the sustainance of the Programme was also examined between the first survey and during the revisit in the study area.

The findings reveal that the implementing agency was preoccupied with reaching its targets only, participation of financial institutions viz., (commercial banks (CBs) and Regional Rual Banks (RRBs)) with the programme implementation show mixed trend, however, RRBs performance seems to be encouraging. Land-linked and non-farm schemes are dominant in the developed and in the backward blocks, respectively. Leakages seems to be very minimal (5%). The bottom group among the rural poor of the economic category fair better participation with the programme and also helps in recycling of loan amount than other groups. The zonal peculiarities and the priorities of the beneficiaries not considered at the time of sanctioning of the schemes. The Incremental Capital Output Ratio (ICOR) was higher in the backward blocks than in the developed blocks. Diversification of the rural economy through IRDP seem to be marginal. Acceptance level of the non-farm schemes was highly significant in terms of generating income and employment. The intactness of the asset depend on the economic condition and the perspective of the beneficiaries, poor extension services, the linkages, and sustainance of the Programme clearly reveals during revisists.

The policy implications emerges from the study are, the target group is not homogeneous and sanctioning of the scheme uniformly would make no sense unless otherwise identified the poor with specific criterion. The implementing agency should be well versed with the regional peculiarities. RRBs with sufficient staff, funds etc., and involving panchayatraj institutions, VOs and NGOs right from identification of beneficiaries down to financing and monitoring of the programme was called for, supporting services like marketing of the product, providing working capital and raw-materials required to be looked into, selected list of the beneficiaries should be kept on the panchayat / mandal office notice board and published in the local news papers / pamplets, to prevent selling of the animal husbandry schemes during droughts fodder banks should be opened and accessibility over Common Property Resources (CPRs) should be made available for the rural poor in the normal circumstances. Added to this care should be taken to provide timely veterinary facilities in villages.

S. Erappa

Acknowledgements

It is a great pleasure for me to acknowledge here the contribution and help rendered by many people in the completion of this research work.

Ever since I joined the Institute for Social and Economic Change (ISEC), Bangalore, research issues concerning poverty interested me enormously. Incidentally my participation as member of the research team under the supervision of Prof. V. M. Rao, Head, Rural Economics Unit, ISEC, in the Concurrent Evaluation Survey (CES) project on Integrated Rural Development Programme (IRDP) during 1985-86 gave me an opportunity to learn about the extent of deprivations among the target groups in rural Karnataka. After completing this project Prof. V. M. Rao undertook a World Bank Sponsored Project on Rural Poor in Karnataka. I have also participated as member of the research team and reviewed the literature in the universities and research organisations on Anti-Poverty Programmes implemented by Government of Karnataka and Voluntary Organisations on rural poor in Karnataka. In the former project I benefited profusely through field work experience and in the case of latter project, my learning process was enriched by reviewing the literature on rural poverty. With this background and at the suggestion and encouragement of Professor V. M. Rao the present study was undertaken. The incisive comments and suggestions of Dr. V. M. Rao, Dr. G.Thimmaiah, Dr. H. G. Hanumappa, Prof.S.N.Nanje Gowda, Dr. R.G. Desai, Dr. D.T.Nanje Gowda, Dr. N.Rajasekharan and Dr. H. S. Shylendra, has helped me in the completion of this research work. In this context, I am highly grateful and indebted to all of them. I am also grateful to the two anonymous referees of this research work for their valuable comments and suggestions.

My deep sense of gratitude is due to Prof. G. Thimmaiah former Director (now Chairman, State Finance Commission, Government of Karnataka) and Sri T. R. Satish Chandran, Director, ISEC for his constant encouragement for their constant encouragement and remainders to complete this work.

The secondary data collected from the records of the relevant departments of Government of Karnataka in general and particularly Department of Rural Development in Bangalore and concerned staff members of the District Rural Development Agency, Block Development Officers and Banks in the study area. It is a pleasure to express my sincere thanks to all of them for their co-operation. I would like to thank the selected heads of IRDP beneficiary households who readily spared their time in furnishing the relevant information and also the concerned village panchayat office staff members for furnishing information on the selected villages.

It was my interaction with the respondents during CES and Revisits (1990-91) which helped me in understanding the issues concerning implementation of IRDP on the one hand, and on the other, the perception of the rural poor households of who availed IRD programme in rural India.

I am also thankful to ISEC library staff for their help. Besides my thanks are also due to Sri Krishna Chandran for his help in computing of data, Sri T. Amarnath for his painstaking effort in typing the drafts and final version of this work; and for Sri Lingaraju for preparing the study area map.

Last but not the least I am grateful to my parents, my wife - Prema, who tolerated discomforts and patiently encouraged me in completing this work as well as many other research pursuits. My children Arun and Manu deserve special thanks for their keeness in my work and their sacrifice for my absence from them.

S. Erappa

Contents

Contents

1

Introduction

Poverty exists in the developed as well as developing countries. It manifests itself either in the form of relative poverty, which is predominently seen in the developed countries or in the form of absolute poverty which prevails in the developing and under-developed countries. While the former one is tolerable, the latter affects the most vulnerable sections of the society who do not command the basic goods and services. These sections are called by different nomenclature, like weaker sections, vulnerable groups, target groups, rural poor.

The disillusionment about the concept of growth as an indicator of economic progress, particularly in the context of Third World countries, has led policy makers as well as many researchers to look for a much more broad-based frame to understand and analyse the socio-economic and related processes. In this regard, the concept of development became quite relevant. Studying the processes of socio-economic change in terms of overall development provided meaningful insights, as compared to studying the economic level of a country in terms of growth as represented by changes in the Gross National Product (GNP). The main reason for this was too much emphasis laid on economic infrastructure like installation of heavy industries, and power generation projects, in the planning process. Also, the pattern of allocation of investment was rather 'urban biased' and the rural areas were deprived of resources (Michael Lipton: 1978). As a result, the job creation in other than capital intensive sectors declined (ILO : 1977). Development economists like Dudley Seers (1972), Haq (1976), Meier (1964, 1984) envisaged the importance of economic development over economic growth. Despite the failure of the trickle down theory, many emphasised that rapid economic growth alone can take care of poverty alleviation.

Several studies revealed that GNP is positively correlated with increase in inequalities (Irving Kravis : 1960, Simon Kuznets : 1976, Harry Oshima : 1962). During the process of modernization, inequalities are bound to increase in the under-developed countries. But in the developed countries, an increase in the Gross Domestic Product (GDP) results in the reduction of inequalities (Kuznets : 1976, Paukert : 1973). This trend is called the inverted 'U' hypothesis. Later on, the 'U' hypothesis was questioned, based on the reliability of the data and the methodology adopted (Saith : 1983).

Development is a very complex phenomenon encompassing a number of socio-economic and related factors. Hence, studies conducted to understand the processes of economic development had to be inter-disciplinary in nature. But in this context, in the Third World countries, with a majority of their population depending on agriculture and again a majority of them being poor, economic factors outweighed others. This is not to indicate that non-economic factors had no influence on the levels of living or on the levels of development in poor countries. Studies dealing with development have tried to treat both economic and non-economic factors, as far as possible, on an equal footing for analysing different issues. Many of these studies have also offered several policy options to combat the problems faced by the Third World countries.

The components (non-income factors) of Physical Quality of Life Index (PQLI) like infant mortality, life expectancy and basic literacy are important to assess a particular nation's performance in providing the basic needs of the people (Gerald Meier : 1986). The absolute poverty explains the level of deprivation of the basic needs, which can be seen predominantly in Third World nations. The above indicators, however, are more appropriate for inter- country comparison in terms of level of development rather than levels of income of the people.

One of the ways to unfold the complexities of development processes is to understand the impact of some of the developmental programmes which are expected to transform the living conditions of the poorer sections of the population. In this context, it is important to raise certain questions like "who are the poor?", "why are they poor?", "can special programmes for the poor bring in the desired change?". For answering these questions, one has not only to analyse the content of the special programmes, but also look at these programmes from the point of view of the beneficiaries. Further, one may have to study and analyse a number of economic and non-economic factors which are at work to bring about the desired rural transformation through various anti-poverty programmes. An attempt is made in the following to understand the concept of poverty from various angles. Such an attempt, it is hoped, will enable one to capture the meaning of this concept in all its ramifications.

Keeping these in view, an attempt is made to classify broadly the available literature on the concept of poverty into four different schools of thought:

1. Socio-economic Deprivation
2. Nutritional Issues
3. Household Income and Consumption Expenditure Issues, and
4. Structural Problems.

1. SOCIO-ECONOMIC DEPRIVATION

The prominent among scholars who advocated this approach are Amartya Sen, Peter Townsend, Paul Streeten, Robert Chambers and others. They highlighted various forms of deprivation (economic, educational, health, social and the like) experienced by the poor.

Deprivation, according to many of these scholars, is the main cause of poverty. In other words, though goods and services are available in the market, the poorer sections in the society cannot afford them. Hence Sen (1987) has rightly pointed out that studying poverty means studying levels of deprivation. To understand the different dimensions of the poverty syndrome, both absolute and relative deprivations should be segregated. The intensity of deprivation can be explained by the wide gap between the incomes of the affluent population and their counterparts (Paul Streeten : 1978).

From the sociological point of view, Peter Townsend (1970) pointed out that poverty 'is a general form of deprivation which is the effect of mal-distribution of resources'. He further pointed out that poverty is mainly a social deprivation, which can be eliminated through social change.

2. NUTRITIONAL ISSUES

The scholars working on issues relating to nutritional aspects of poverty argue that levels of nutrition can serve as an important criterion to measure poverty. Normally, the poorer sections living in under-developed countries suffer from mal-nutrition/under-nutrition. Sukhatme (1965) calculated the minimum food basket, which consists of 0.403 kg. of cereals, 0.104 kg. of pulses, 0.201 kg. of milk, 0.137 kg. of fruits and vegetables and certain quantities of starchy roots, sugar, oils and fats, meat, fish and eggs per day per person. In this context, Sukhatme (1978) revealed that "as income increases, the energy intake increases, rapidly to start with and gradually thereafter, indicating that an appreciable number of people remain under-nourished for want of adequate income". This statement indicates a clear relationship between poverty and undernutrition. The determinants of widespread nutritional deficiencies are (a) inadequate intake of food, (b) family food habits and (c) wide spread prevalence of health disorder (Swaminathan : 1983). The ` primary' poverty as delineated by Rowntree (1941) was attributed to nutritional aspects and diversion of subsistence level income to purchase other than the basic requirements. Rowntree's minimum nutritional requirement is endorsed by Orshansky (1975) based on his estimates of minimum food expenditure. But, Martin Rein criticised Rowntree's definition as arbitrary and concludes that ` subsistence measures of poverty cannot claim to rest solely on a technical or scientific definition of nutritional adequacy. Values, preference and political realities influence the definition of subsistence'.

3. HOUSEHOLD INCOME AND CONSUMPTION EXPENDITURE ISSUES

A number of studies considered income as the main indicator to assess the level of poverty of a household. With the help of income-tax statistics and national sample survey data, many researchers (Uma Datta Roy Chowdhury : 1977, Bhatty : 1974) measured income inequalities. The available data are inadequate because they do not furnish many other details like all the sources of income and disposable income. The skewed distribution of income mainly helps to arrive at relative poverty irrespective of different income levels and the extent of deprivation in the case of lower bottom group (Bhatty : 1974). Simon Kuznets (1974) indicates that "in a meaningful distribution of income by size, the recipient unit has to be a family or household and cannot be a person ... the conventional distribution of incomes among the families or households by income per family or household make little sense, since they are affected by changing different inequalities among families or households by size". To examine Kuznets' statements empirically, Hanumappa (1978) considered three characteristics of the household viz. size of the sample families, educational levels of the heads of households and other workers in the households and occupational status of heads of households as well as of all workers in the households, to determine the levels of income. Scholars and institutions have relied on income and expenditure data to arrive at the proportion of population living below a certain minimum defined income/expenditure level, known as poverty line.

The concept of 'poverty line' is accepted to estimate the incidence of poverty in the developing countries. However, there is no single accepted definition of 'poverty line.' (Victor Fuchs : 1967, Mollie Orshansky : 1968, Michael Harrington : 1968). To have a single accepted definition of poverty line may not be possible because of various reasons like age, sex, climate and variations in the intake of calories by the people. Estimates have been made of the magnitude of poverty by different organisations and scholars in India also. Table 1.1 gives the details of the estimates made on the basis of the poverty line to arrive at the percentage of rural population living below the poverty line. The magnitude of poverty, however, varies from one study to another. It ranged between 40 per cent in 1960-61 and 50.7 % in 1980-85 (Table 1.1).

Table 1.1 : A Comparative Statement Showing different estimates of Rural Poverty in India

S. No.	Year	Organisation/ Researcher	Estimated No. of poor (Millions)	% of rural population below poverty line	Definition of Poverty based on
1	2	3	4	5	6
1.	1960-61	Dandekar & Ruth	135.0	40.0	Rs. 1.80 p.c.c.e. at 1960-61 prices yielding a minimum of 2,250 calories per day.
		Ahluwalia[9]	152.0	42.0	Rs. 189 p.c.c.e., p.a., at 1960-61 prices.
		Vaidyanathan[10]	213.5	59.5	Rs. 240 p.c.c.e., p.a., at 1960-61 prices.
		Ojha	184.2	51.8	Rs. 216 p.c.c.e., p.a., at 1960-61 prices.
2.	1961-62	Ahluwalia	157.0	42.3	Rs. 180 p.c.c.e., p.a., at 1960-61 prices.
3.	1962-63	NIRD	166.0	44.9	The regression equation between NDP from agriculture and Ahluwalia's time series estimates of incidence of poverty.
4.	1963-64	E P W de Costa	161.0	34.6	Three types of classification —destitutes, severe destitutes and the poor—based on minimum per capita expenditure per annum.
		B S Minhas[11]	221.0	57.8	Two alternative levels of Rs. 240 and Rs. 2.00 per capita annual consumption expenditure at 1960-61 prices.
		Ahluwalia	189.0	49.1	Above-mentioned criterion.
5.	1964-65	Vaidyanathan	235.7	60.0	As mentioned above (Rs. 240 p.c.p.a., c.e.)

Contd.....

Table 1.1 : (Contd.)

1	2	3	4	5	6
		Bardhan[12]	174.4	51.6	180 p.c., c.e, p.a. at 1960-61 prices
		Ahluwalia	198.0	50.4	Above-mentioned criterion.
6.	1965-66	Ahluwalia	205.0	51.1	Above-mentioned criterion
7.	1966-67	Ahluwalia	235.0	57.4	Above-mentioned criterion.
8.	1967-68	Ahluwalia	241.0	57.9	Above-mentioned criterion
		Dandekar and Ruth	166.4	40.0	Above-mentioned criterion.
		Vaidyanathan	—	67.8	Above-mentioned criterion.
		Minhas	210.0	50.6	Rs. 240 p.c.c.e., p.a.
		Ojha	289.0	70.0	Estimates of minimum desirable income i.e., Rs.216 to Rs. 480 per annum.
9.	1968-69	Ahluwalia	227.0	53.5	Above-mentioned criterion.
10.	1969-70	AFICCI	218.3	41.2	Rs. 240 p.c., c.e., p.a. at 1960-61 prices.
		NIRD	196.0	46.2	Earlier mentioned criterion.
11.	1970-71	Ahluwalia	217.0	49.1	Earlier mentioned criterion.
		II PC*	198.9	45.0	Rs. 336 p.c.c.e., p.a.
12.	1971-72	NIRD	183.0	41.5	Earlier mentioned criterion.
13.	1972-73	NIRD	212.0	47.2	Earlier mentioned criterion.
		Planning Commission**(Draft Five Year Plan)	200.0	35.6	Rs.480 p.c.c.e., p.a. at 1972-73 prices.
14.	1973-74	Ahluwalia	221.0	47.6	Earlier mentioned criterion.
		IIPO	208.0	44.8	Rs. 516 p.c., c.c., p.a.
15.	1974-75	NIRD	232.0	50.1	Earlier mentioned criterion.
16.	1975-76	NIRD[14]	225.0	47.7	Earlier mentioned criterion.
17.	1976-77	NIRD[15]	216.0	45.2	Earlier mentioned criterion.
18.	1977-78	Planning Commission	251.7	50.8	Rs. 741.60 p.c., c.a., p.a. (2,400 calories p.c. per day)
		IIPO[17]	246.4	50.8	Rs.780 p.c., c.a., p.a. (2,400 calories p.c. per day)

Contd......

Table 1.1 : (Contd.)

1	2	3	4	5	6
19.	1980-85	Planning[16] Commission	259.6	50.7	Rs. 76 per person per month at current prices (2,400 calories p.c. per day)

* Refers to 1971; ** Refers to 1973;
p.c.c.e.= Per capita Consumer Expenditure; p.a. = Per annum.

Source : Mohan Lal (1988), p. 12–15.

4. STRUCTURAL PROBLEMS

The studies dealing with the structure of the economy mainly envisage the delineation of the poor based on the distribution pattern of land holdings, asset structure and agricultural production. According to them, poverty is the result of unequal distribution of various assets, particularly land.

The quantum of land owned determines the household's socio-economic status in rural India. Based on the NSS data, scholars like Minhas (1974), Bhardhan (1986), Vaidyanathan (1974) and Dandekar and Rath (1971a) have drawn interesting findings to highlight how the structural variables like land activate or mitigate and are also responsible for the perpetuation of rural poverty in the country. Bhatty (1974) arrived at the incidence of rural poverty by considering occupational groups, viz., agricultural labourers, cultivators, non-agricultural labourers by using Sen's poverty index and Head Count method. The incidence of poverty was very high among agricultural labourers, as compared to the other occupational categories.

Thus, conceptually, poverty has been visualised as a phenomenon which arises due to factors like socio-economic deprivation, inability to have minimum food requirements arising out of low levels of income and also inequitable distribution of productive assets.

THIRD WORLD NATIONS' EXPERIENCE ON POVERTY ALLEVIATION

Though poverty prevails in all countries, its magnitude is much higher in developing countries and efforts are being made at different levels (i.e., regional, national and international) to alleviate absolute levels of poverty. The World Development Report (1992, 25) says that "more than 1 billion people today live in abject poverty.... Alleviating poverty is both morally imperative and essential for environmental sustainability". Table 1.2 shows the incidence of poverty in the developing world. About 30 per cent of the world's population is poor. The percentage of population below the poverty line is much higher in South Asian and Sub-Saharan African nations.

Table 1.2 : Poverty in Developing World

Region	Percentage of population below the poverty line		Number of (millions)	
	1985	1990	1985	1990
All developing countries	30.5	29.7	1051	1133
South Asia	51.8	49.0	532	562
East Asia	13.2	11.3	182	169
Sub-Saharan Africa	47.6	47.8	184	216
Middle East & North Africa	30.6	33.1	60	73
Eastern Europe	7.1	7.1	5	5
Latin America and the Caribbean	22.4	25.5	87	108

Source: World Development Report 1992, Development and the Environment, Oxford University Press, New York, Table 1.1, P 30.

Among the world's rural poor, most of them (more than 500 millions) are found in Asian countries. The incidence is in alarming proportions in these countries. For instance, Bangladesh (80 per cent), India (37.5 per cent), Pakistan (35 per cent to 45 per cent) Sri Lanka (14 per cent) and Indonesia (14 per cent) have considerable proportion of poor people.

To reduce the incidence of rural poverty, several rural development strategies were evolved in countries like India. The strategies evolved for rural development are given in Table 1.3. Broadly, these strategies are grouped under four categories viz., Technocratic, Reformist, Radical and Free Market Determined (Lea and

Table 1.3 : Approaches to Rural Development Strategies

Rural Deve-lopment	Major Objectives of the Policy Makers	Major Bene-ficiaries	Dominant form of Tenure	Examples from Case Studies
Techno cratic	Increase output	Land owning elite	Large private farms Plantations, estates & various tenancy systems co-existing with large farms dominanting.	Phili-ppines
Reformist	Redistribute income (& wealth) increase increase output, social change	Middle peasant 'Progressive' farmers and spe-cific ethnic groups	Family farms, co-operative and land settlement schemes	PNG, Tanzania, Malaysia, Sri Lanka
Radical	Social Change: Re-distribute political power, wealth and output	Small Peasants and landless labourers	Collectives, Comm-unes and State Farms	China, Vietnam
Free Market Deteri-mined	Increase Output and create investible surplus for develop-ment	Large Farmers capitalist sub-sectors in rural areas	Owner-operated large farms	Indonesia Bangla-desh South Korea

Source: Rural Development and the State: David A M Lea and D P Chaudhuri Contributions and Dilemmas in Developing Countries, (ed), 1983, p. 24.

Chaudhuri : 1983). The details based on the above approaches against the spelt out objectives, the major beneficiaries, type of farms and the country adopted are identified by the authors. By and large, all the four rural development strategies aim at increasing the output. Both the reformist and the radical strategies go beyond the output oriented approach and are targetted to achieve social justice and equity through the redistribution of income or wealth. Hence, the beneficiaries covered are middle and small farmers and landless agricultural labourers. These strategies are accepted and implemented in countries like China, Sri Lanka and Malaysia. (Table 1.3).

Whereas, the other two strategies viz., technocratic and free market determined, which depend on technology and market force to a large extent benefited the large farmers, which resulted in establishing private operated large farms and their polarization, in countries like Philippines, Indonesia, Bangladesh and South Korea.

Table 1.4 exhibits the details of typology of strategies of rural development programmes designed and implemented to overcome the poverty nexus. The reformist model and radical model are mainly targetted at rural areas through the labour intensive approach to bring out social change in the rural population in general and rural poor in particular. But there may be little deviations like the small farm size (Reformist Model) and large farm size (Collective Model) this approach was also followed in Taiwan, Japan, China and part of Tanzania. Countries adopting radical and reformist models could overcome the problem of poverty much faster than the other nations. Such of those countries which adopted free

Table 1.4 : A Typology of Strategies of Rural Development Programmes

	Reformist Model	Free Market Model	Technocratic-Model	Collectives Model
Farm Size	Small	Usually Large	Policy Determined	Large
Land System	Owner/Cultivator	Private and Commercial	Private	Social Control
Technology	Labour intensive	Market-induced	Policy-induced	Socially determined
Non-Agricultural sub-sector	High/Small policy determined	Small	Small	High/Small socially determined
Employment mode prices	Unpaid Family Labour policy determined	Wage based determined	Wage-based policy determined to keep profitability high	Share-based Internally consistent state-determined
Agricultural Input supply	Local/urban policy determined	Urban	Urban	Local
Marketing	Co-operative	Private	Private/co-operative	Co-operative
Rural Institutions	Socially determined with state help	Market determined	Policy determined	Socially determined
Successful examples (from policy makers' point of view)	Taiwan, Japan	Pakistan Punjab, parts of Brazil	Indian Punjab, South Korea	China, parts Tanzania

Source: Rural Development and the State: David A M Lea and D P Chaudhuri (ed), 1983, p. 19.

market model and technocratic model like India and Pakistan are still to accomplish the goal of poverty eradication.

Initially, the Pakistan Government introduced the Village Agricultural and Industrial Development Programme, the Basic Democracies System and the Rural Works Programmes to eradicate poverty in the country. The Integrated Rural Development Programme was introduced later on because of the failure of the earlier programmes (Anwar et al. : 1982).

The Malaysian experience to combat poverty through anti-poverty programmes resulted in the non-poor benefiting to a greater extent than the needy (ILO : 1979). Similarly, in the Philippines, though overall growth has been visible the incidence of poverty increased (Bussink : 1980) and the standard of living of the rural poor declined (Azizur Rahman Khan : 1977). Interestingly, in China, apart from land reforms, rural relief and welfare programmes were initiated in 1949. The Welfare programme covering five-guarantees (food, clothing, fuel, a proper burial and school fee) was implemented through-out the country (Deborah Davis & Friedman : 1978). As a result, China could successfully alleviate rural poverty and solve unemployment problem.

The Cooperative capitalism with subsidised modern inputs introduced in Bangladesh to eradicate poverty helped the rural elite group rather than the landless and the poor (Azizur Rahman Khan: 1979). Muhammad Yunus (1988) initiated Grameen Bank in Bangladesh during 1976. The establishment of 400 branches of the Grameen Bank enabled to cover 4 lakh IRDP beneficiaries (82 per cent women beneficiaries to total). But the area covered by these branches was very small (i.e., 8.5 per cent of the villages out of a total of 68,000 villages). The loans given by the Grameen Bank resulted in 35 per cent increase in the per capita income of the rural poor households. The recycle of the bank money (repayment made by the beneficiaries) through 'bankers on bike' accounted for 97 per cent in Grameen bank which was very much higher than the local private banks i.e. 27 per cent (Judith Tendler : 1987, Norman Uphoff : 1986).

LAND REFORMS

In countries which adopted radical methodology initially, eradication of poverty was thought to be achieved by correcting the structural disorder through land reforms. The main objective of land reforms are:to promote the goals of self-employment for the rural poor, reduce inequality, alleviate rural poverty and attain higher output. It was expected that social equity and productivity could go hand in hand if land reforms were effectively implemented.

Several Third World nations initiated and implemented land reforms in different years. The Republic of Korea and Japan initiated distribution of land together with promoting labour intensive activities on land which helped in overcoming the problem of poverty permanently. Similarly, China and Taiwan have succeeded in reducing poverty and inequality quite considerably (Keith Griffen : 1988) through land reforms. Several governments tried to eradicate poverty by correcting the structural disorder through structural/fundamental reforms by the process of reducing the ceiling limits through legislation. The surplus land was acquired and distributed to the landless.

The outcome of a seminar on land reforms and rural development held at the National Institute of Rural Development, Hyderabad indicates that "effective implementation of land reforms could contribute to efficient functioning of markets and would facilitate the shift to a non-subsidised agricultural growth, while simultaneously contributing to the goals of improved employment and equity" (Haque and Parthasarathy : 1992, 397). But the Working Group (1989) expressed that "the land reforms programme has virtually come to a dead end... it is, however, widely believed that land reforms have really not been sincerely and effectively implemented.... There have been virtually no new initiatives which would bring land reforms back to the front stage of social and economic development" (Ministry of Agriculture : 1989, 1). Major lacunae like lack of interest by the political leaders to implement the land reforms, not conferring the ownership right on the tenants and modern inputs not being used by the share croppers resulted in land grab movements in Andhra Pradesh (G Parthsarathy : 1992). The above few reasons, however, are responsible for the failure of land reforms in accomplishing the objectives.

POVERTY ALLEVIATION PROGRAMMES—THE INDIAN EXPERIENCE

In the Indian context, poverty is basically a rural phenomenon because a little less than 80 per cent of the population lives in the rural area. India has about 14 per cent of the world's population and her share among the developing countries is 24.5 per cent. The UNDP,in its Human Development Report (1991), has also mentioned that nearly 410 million people in India were poor in 1990. Since Independence, various rural development programmes have been designed and implemented to eradicate poverty in the country.

Generally, the target groups are demarcated into economic groups (small and marginal farmers, landless labourers, and rural artisans) and social groups (Scheduled Caste and Scheduled Tribes). To uplift the target group, the Five Year Plans have aimed at achieving improvement in productivity, reducing pressure on land, industrial development, economic growth, self reliance, social justice and poverty eradication.

The implementation of anti-poverty programmes in India during the last 15 years provides an interesting ground for undertaking research to find out the type of rural transformation that has taken place as a result of some of these special programmes.

In the first three Plans it was assumed that economic growth through the operation of the trickle down theory would take care of the problem of poverty. The Community Development Programme was the first of its kind started nation wide in October 1952, with the principle of self-help supported by government funding and guidance (Mukerji : 1967, Taylor et al. : 1967). The National Extension Service and Intensive Agriculture District Programme (IADP) were introduced to provide extension services to government programmes and a sectoral approach, particularly to agriculture, respectively. Further, to increase food production, Intensive Agricultural Area Development (IAAP) and High Yielding Varieties Programmes (HYV) were mooted in successive years. What was expected from the above programmes was not realised due to many socio-economic factors.

From the Fourth Plan onwards, the 'special programme strategy was given importance through Small Farmers Development Agency (SFDA), Marginal Farmers and Agricultural labourers Development Agency (MFALDA) and Drought-prone Area Programme (DPAP) which aimed at generating income and employment of farm and non-farm activities. Nevertheless, these programmes were also beset with problems like wrong identification of beneficiaries, inadequate inputs availability, lack of forward and backward linkages, and lack of co-ordination between the departments concerned to implement the programme (Laxminarayana : 1973, Deshing Raj : 1987). In addition, area development programmes like Hill Area Development Programme, Command Area Development Programme and whole Village Development Programme were devised during the Fifth Five Year Plan.

In the Sixth Five Year Plan, direct attack on poverty was envisaged through Integrated Rural Development Programme (IRDP), a beneficiary oriented programme introduced in 1978 by merging SFDA and MFAL. IRDP was aimed at providing economically productive assets to generate additional income and employment (self-employment) to the weaker sections in the society. The employment programmes like National Rural Employment Programme (NREP) and Rural Landless Employment Guarantee Programme (RLEGP) were introduced to provide employment opportunities during the slack agricultural season and also to create infrastructure base in the rural areas. Later on, these employment programmes are merged and called Jawahar Rozgar Yojana (JRY) to overcome certain drawbacks like non-payment of minimum wages, delay in payment of wages, middlemen and contractors' exploitation (Department of Rural Development, Government of India : 1989).

The combined efforts of economic development and anti-poverty programmes reduced the incidence of poverty in the country. Table 1.5 indicates the incidence of poverty level over a period of time.

The incidence of rural poverty has come down from 54.1 per cent in 1972-73 to 33.4 per cent in 1987-88. The percentage of total population living below the poverty line has declined from 51.5 per cent to 29.9 per cent during the same period. The estimates made by the Expert Group on the proportions and number of the poor are slightly higher than the Planning Commission estimates (Table 1.5).

One relevant issue in this context is to find out why poverty accentuates, and affects the life of the target group. The anti-poverty programmes (APPs) devised and implemented seem to be more relief- oriented or welfare-oriented in nature (V M Rao : 1988). The implementation of APPs appears to be *ad hoc* and IRDP seems to be a soft approach (Rao and Erappa : 1987). While

Table 1.5 : Estimates of Incidence of Poverty

(percentage)

Sectors	% of Population Living Below Poverty Line							
	1972-73		1977-78		1983-84		1987-88	
	PC	EG	PC	EG	PC	EG	PC	EG
Rural	54.1	56.4*	51.2	53.1	40.4	45.6	33.4	39.1
Urban	41.2	49.2*	38.2	47.4	28.1	42.2	20.1	40.1
All India	51.5	54.9*	48.3	51.8	37.4	44.8	29.2	39.3

Note : PC : Planning Commission, EG : Expert Group on Estimates of Proportion and Number of Poor.
: The reference year was 1973-74.

Source : (a) Planning Commission, Government of India, quoted in Economic Survey 1993-94, Government of India, Table 9.4, p.148.
(b) Planning Commission : Report of the Expert Group on Estimates of Proportion and Number of Poor, July 1993, quoted in Economic Survey 1993-94, Government of India, Table 9.5, p.148.

examining the inherent qualities of the rural poor, Myrdal (1970) pointed out that the target groups are mostly passive, apathetic and inarticulate. Similarly, Marx had identified that the lower bottom people in the society do not have either organising ability or strong will power.

INTEGRATED RURAL DEVELOPMENT PROGRAMME (IRDP)

IRDP is a major anti-poverty programme devised to alleviate rural poverty in India through direct attack. IRDP was launched in 1977-78 and initially covered 16 selected districts in the country. Later on, on 2nd October 1980 it was extended to all the 5011 administrative blocks in the country. The prime objective of IRDP is to identify the target group to provide them productive assets and skills which help in generating additional income and employment opportunities and in turn helping them to cross the official poverty line. The schemes sanctioned under IRDP are in the areas of agriculture, trading, village industries, animal husbandry and services.

The main thrust of IRDP is to utilise locally available resources and to integrate sectoral programmes to achieve growth, eradicate poverty and unemployment of the rural poor.

IRDP is being implemented through District Rural Development Agency (DRDA) at the district level. Block Development Officers (BDO) and the staff members are involved in the preliminary works like identification of beneficiaries, processing the application forms, and the Chief Secretary who heads the Co-ordination Committee monitors the over-all implementation of IRDP at the State level. The funds for the IRDP have been shared by Central and State governments on 50 : 50 basis. The main aspect of IRDP is the capital subsidy given to beneficiaries along with institutional loans. The subsidy varies from 25 per cent to 50 per cent of the total unit cost of the scheme i.e. for small farmers it is 25 per cent, for marginal farmers and landless labourers, it is 33.3 per cent and for scheduled caste and scheduled tribes beneficiaries, it is 50 per cent (Government of India, IRDP Manual : 1987). Out of the total beneficiaries assisted, SC/STs and women beneficiaries should constitute 30 per cent.

The identification of the rural poor under IRDP is done mainly on the basis of the poverty line which is revised from time to time, keeping in mind the rising prices. It was Rs.3,500 (per family per annum) during the Sixth Plan and increased to Rs.6,400 during the Seventh Plan and then further to Rs.11,060 during the Eight Plan. Nearly 35 million households had received assistance under IRDP till the end of the Seventh Five Year Plan.

2

Review of Literature

In this chapter an attempt is made to review the available literature. The first part of this review attempts to trace the roots of the debate on poverty in a historical perspective and the second part concentrates on a review of literature concerning attempts to alleviate poverty in rural areas in recent times through programmes like IRDP. However, it may be mentioned that the review attempted here is more of an illustrative nature, as exhaustive coverage of studies has not been possible.

SECTION I

This section deals with the contributions made by economists to the literature on poverty.

Historically the Mercantilists viewed poverty as an useful and indeed essential prerequsite to augment the wealth of the country. They felt that the bulk of the population should be kept under conditions of poverty. This view reflects the degree of contempt of the members of the ruling and upper classes for the common man. Arthur Young (quoted in Rimlinger : 1976) viewed as late as 1771, that "Everyone but an idiot knows that the lower classes must be kept poor or they will never be industrious" They also went on to state that the people of the lower classes were crude, ignorant, and inclined to disorderly behaviour and idleness. They inferred that only constant pressure of misery saved them from idleness which is the mother of all vices. Mandeville (quoted in Rimlinger : 1976) noted that "there is a vast number of journey-men... who, by four days labour in a week they can maintain themselves, will hardly be persuaded to work the fifth". The mercantilists also held the view that high wages are equivalent to low production.

The harsh judgement against the lower classes in the Mercantilist epoch has been tampered by the rise of humanism in the second half of the 18th century. Adam Smith, though the main proponent of this view, had regarded the ordinary labourer much more important than the merchants, politicians, and the rich and well-to-do as a class. He felt that drunkenness, the main background of the common man, was "a consequence of circumstances, rather than an indication of innate character defect" (Adam Smith: 1776, 1976, 343). He further asserted that "the difference of natural talents in different men is, in reality, much less than we are aware of; and the very different genius which appears to distinguish men of different proportions... is not upon many occasions so much the cause, on the effect of the division of labour" (Adam Smith 1776, 1976, 15).

Contrary to Mercantilists, Smith felt that ordinary people had stricter moral standards and were more industrious than the rich. Again, in contrast to the mercantilists' doctrine of "Utility of Poverty" he declared that "the wages of labour are the encouragement of industry.... A plentiful subsistence increases the bodily strength of the labourer and the comfortable hope of bettering his condition, and of ending his days perhaps in ease and plenty, animates him to exert that strength to the utmost. Where wages are high, accordingly... the workmen are more active, diligent and expeditious, than where they are low" (Adam Smith : 1776, 1976, 81). He also exhibited, in contrast, that the high income of the rich was often detrimental to national welfare. He again argued that where the workers and landlords are well off, one finds a happy and prosperous country. But he argued that the rate of profit varies inversely with national prosperity.

Having realised the problems of the poor, Smith argued for the solution that education benefits society, because, it is conducive to greater domestic peace. He wrote that "the more the lower orders are instructed, the less liable they are to the delusions of enthusiasm and superstition, which, among ignorant nations, frequently occasion the most dreadful disorder...." (Adam Smith : 1776, 1976, 142). Smith was highly critical of the laws of wages and prices. He opined that "laws concerning wages and prices were always either equitable or in favour of the employers. The masters would never be at a disadvantage because they were the councilors of the legislatures.

Smith was in favour of public regulation to have favourable welfare effects. The law should make the masters to pay their workers in money, not in goods. The prices of necessities, such as bread, should be regulated, where their supply was controlled by monopolies. He felt that the poor would be better off facing the pitfalls of Laissez-faire than the handicaps of regulation.

These arguments of Smith motivated the government to help the poor and support the weak. It was a subject of heated debates from one group of economists, particularly from Ricardo to Malthus through their theories of distribution and population, respectively. Malthus (1820, 1914 : 48) argued that "The Poor laws of England tend to depress the general condition of the poor. Their first and obvious tendency is to increase the population without increasing the food for its support...." Ricardo felt that this unwarranted increase in population could only force an extension of the margin of cultivation which, given the assumption of diminishing returns, would put an inevitable upward pressure on the price of food and a downward pressure on the general level of real wages. Apart from this, they found that the Government's attempt to help the poor is to violate the laws of nature and the freedom of the individual. Malthus, as in Karma theory of Indian Veda, wanted nature to take its own course and punish those who do not know how to take care of themselves without Government help.

In the last quarter of the last century, taking suggestion from Adam Smith and Ricardo, Henry George (1879, 1981), Karl Marx and Marshall debated the pros and cons of nationalisation and privatisation (Rajasekaran, p.2). Like Marx, Henry George claimed that as long as land is privately owned, prosperity would increase poverty and called for the fiscal remedy of a 'single tax' to appropriate land rent, while Marshall (1891) argued that poverty was a temporary phenomenon caused by a population that was too big in number but too low in skills; and advocated "taming" competition by education, charity, thrift and breeding limitation. Both George and Marshall regarded economic progress as necessary but not sufficient for the good life. But they differed in the sufficiency part, for George, sufficiency conditions involved redistributing land rents, while Marshall required educating the population and inculcating habits of thrift and restraint in breeding. Again they went on to state that poverty is the major source of moral degradation, a society rich enough to eliminate material poverty could achieve in spiritual wealth as well.

Though both George and Marshall got along in so many views, they also differ on many counts. By actual progress, George meant not uplifting the poor, but rather increasing their want, while to Marshall progress had temporarily worsened the plight of the poor, but was dramatically improving their lot along with that of the rest of the society.

George maintains that population growth increases the average productivity of labour even without any technological advances because, "with every additional pair of hands which increasing population brings, there is a more proportionate addition to the productive power of labour". He was also convinced that population growth can seldom reduce the average production of wealth. He was too clear in his mind that this growth in average increased the income of the landlords rather than the labourers. George had a strong solution for this in ` single tax' on land rent, not directly on nationalisation of land. He felt that the indirect taxation would fall upon everybody irrespective of the labourers and landlords and ultimately it (indirect taxation) provokes poverty instead of reducing it.

Contrary to George's view of population growth, Marshall asserts that population growth promotes growth of unskilled labourers and on supply and demand analysis in a competitive framework since there are too many workers, their marginal productivity is low and in turn they are paid less. Marshall also went on to state that in a developing society the evil of poverty is cumulative because poor parents are prevented by their poverty from investing capital in the education and training of their children who are imperfectly fed and clothed (Rajasekaran p.5). He also pinpointed low wages and low levels of education as the major causes of poverty in his three lectures in 1883.

The debate on growth and redistributive policies got deviated to interventionist approach by the world depression of 1930's. As a major proponent of anti-depression policies, Keynes slipped into the area of eliminating poverty too. He identified four factors which were important to eliminate poverty: (1) Power to control population growth, (2) ability to avoid wars, (3) the willingness to trust science and (4) the rate of capital accumulation. His main view was how to increase wages and thereby living standards. Keynes felt that in the long-run, wages head towards the minimum subsistence level. Thus the policy conclusion is that nothing can be done to increase real wages; therefore, nothing can be done to reduce poverty.

Though he was skeptical about overcoming poverty, Keynes had in mind primarily increased social security and pension payments to improve the standard of living of elderly families and individuals. He had the contention that poverty can arise either from a shortage of resources or from the viability to put resources to work and he had the solution in putting the existing idle resources to work.

Deviating from these discussions of poverty and anti-poverty policies, economists like Nurkse, (1953) and Myrdal (1968) have conceptualised poverty as a vicious circle or circular causation. In other words, it is a low level equilibrium trap and how to come out of the trap.

Nurkse (1953, 4) elucidated "vicious circle of poverty as a circular constellation of forces tending to act and react upon one another in such a way as to keep a poor country in a state of poverty". The main circular constellation to Nurkse is physical weakness of the poor. He inferred that a country is poor because it is poor.

To come out of the low level equilibrium of economic stagnation, Nurkse had the solution in making the poor become stronger by providing more to eat, and providing the subsistence farmer with modern techniques, irrigation and fertilizers. If it is materialised, Nurkse recoined the proposition "Country is becoming richer because it is less poor and therefore becoming richer".

Though Nurkse explains a causal interdependence between the various factors in the social system even outside the economic factors, it is conceivable that the social and economic system remains in equilibrium. Myrdal responds to this by answering these questions of why in certain cases circular causation perpetuates stagnation, or permits only minor and temporary movements around a low level equilibrium ? and Is the low level equilibrium stagnation 'normal' in any particular sense?

Myrdal (1968), asserts that circular causation is cumulative. Changes in one condition cause changes in one or several other conditions in the same direction or perhaps, other directions too, from the point of view of development.

From these discussions of low level equilibrium trap and how to get out of it, economists quicken the process to perceive the dual structure of the economy and how one sector plays its role on the other for total development. Being the initiator of the debate, Lewis (1954) hypothesised that agricultural progress is a prerequisite for industrial development and in turn, total development. He drew this through three aspects:

(1) it permits agriculture to release part of its labour force for industrial employment while meeting the increasing food needs of the non-agricultural sector.

(2) it raises agricultural incomes, thereby creating the rural purchasing power needed to buy the industrial goods and rural savings which in turn promote industrial investment.

(3) it enables agriculture to supply the major wage good (food) of industrial worker at a favourable price.

Lewis divided the economy into a capitalist or advanced sector and a subsistence sector. The capitalist sector expands by drawing the cheap agricultural labour into its employment.

While Lewis ignored the agricultural sector, it was rediscovered and the structural interdependence of the agricultural and non-agricultural sectors was emphasized in two sector models by Jorgenson and, Ranis and Fei. Whereas Jorgenson assumes a positive productivity for the agricultural labour force, Ranis and Fei assume a marginal product of zero or close to zero. Ranis and Fei exhibited the interaction between the agricultural and non-farm sectors in initiating and accelerating development. Their study starts from an economy's first departure from quasi-stagnation or the initiation of the Rostow's take-off process to one of self-sustaining growth.

Like Lewis and Ranis and Fei, Higgins (1958) was also drawn to this view of agriculture and economic development. His central thesis is that only a rapid change to extensive, mechanised agriculture, with enough industrialisation to absorb the population displaced from the rural sector, will assure a take off into steady growth. He also went on to state about India that the failure to maintain steady growth of agricultural output makes it extremely difficult to obtain steady growth of industrial output, in an economy where the private sector still dominates.

Higgins' contention is that for raising agricultural productivity, a "big push" industrialisation programme should be given top priority. He suggests, "a cumulative improvement in agricultural productivity in a public policy designed to make labour relatively scarce in agriculture by simultaneously shifting to a more mechanised and large-scale agriculture and encouraging a rapid rate of industrialisation". Unlike Lewis, he warns vehemently about the disastrous consequence of industrialisation without an agricultural revolution or neglect of the agricultural sector.

The interdependence between agriculture and industry has been well established in the discussions of Lewis, Ranis and Fei, Benjamin Higgins and others. This also shows how the lopsided growth in one sector would affect the economic condition of labourers, particularly subsistence wage earners, and in turn their poverty. Now the focus has been narrowed down to agriculture and rural poverty, particularly by development economists. The major developments in this direction are trickle down and centre periphery.

Like the earlier debates on poverty alleviation, at the outset the debate started with the relationship between rural poverty and agricultural production. Ahluwalia (1978) demonstrated that an inverse relationship existed between rural poverty and agricultural production (per capita agricultural production). He further asserted that 'trickle down' mechanisms operated in rural India. Saith (1981), contrary to Ahluwalia, exhibited that while rural poverty and fluctuations in agricultural production (around the trend values) were inversely related, fluctuations in consumer prices (around the same trend values) aggravated rural poverty. Saith further asserted that there was a rising residual trend in rural poverty after accounting for the influence of consumer prices. This contrasts with Ahluwalia's finding that there was no residual time trend in rural poverty.

In a recent analysis, Ahluwalia evinced that if agricultural output is lagged the relationship is considerably strengthened. The addition of declined agricultural output weakens the positive effect of prices but does not negate entirely. Ahluwalia concluded that there was no weakening of the 'trickle down' mechanisms with the advent of green revolution technology. Ahluwalia further established that rural poverty was causally linked to the level of agricultural production and fluctuations in the index of consumer prices. He also established that the suddenness of an increase in consumer prices matters more than otherwise (Rajasekaran, p.10).

In the same 'trickle down' vein Raul Prebisch (1959, 1971) postulated the structuralist paradigm centre-periphery. The focus of the structuralist paradigm lies in the proposition that the process of development and under-development is a single process, and that the disparities between centre and periphery are reproduced through trade. Thus, the periphery's development problems are located within the context of the economy as a whole, revealing the holistic nature of structuralism.

From the influence of regional structure on poverty, Hayami and Kikuchi have looked into the internal structure's role in creating poverty through stratifying the society. Stratification has, says Yujiro Hayami and Masao Kikuchi (1981, 123) developed through institutional innovations such as sustenancy (in which, in the Philippines, only those helped with weeding without receiving wages are employed for harvesting and receive the output share on). They go on to infer that "changes in institutional arrangements governing the use of production factors will be induced when disequilibria between the marginal returns and the marginal costs of factor inputs emerge as the result of changes in economic variables, such as, resource endowments and technology, given the institutional rigidity of factor markets; the direction of institutional change will be towards the restoration of equilibria. Nevertheless, the basic factor appears to be the institutional environment and the high degree of social interaction in the village community.

The basic institutional environment has consisted of the traditional moral principles of mutual help and income sharing within the village. Then the peasant stratification based on institutional innovations in the guise of mutual help and income sharing has been the most efficient route to reducing the disequilibria between marginal factor costs and returns in the village community.

This discussion of the views of different economists over the period brings out the evolution of different views. It vividly exhibits the need for different approaches during different periods in continuum. This presents a holistic view of poverty. It gives a clear understanding of poverty as a concept and how to alleviate and eradicate it.

SECTION II

In this section an attempt is made to review the available/existing literature on IRDP which is the main credit based poverty alleviation scheme in India. The main objective is to understand certain general patterns with regard to various issues of credit based poverty alleviation programmes and to arrive at research gaps and issues for the present study.

In order to identify certain meaningful patterns in the results, the studies have been classified into different groups keeping mainly the objective of IRDP in view. The objective of IRDP is to provide the rural poor (defined on the basis of poverty line) with necessary capital for investment to acquire productive assets, take-up self-employment and thereby enable them to improve their household income and eventually cross the poverty line.

The studies have been grouped into six categories on the basis of the following issues:

(1) Coverage of rural poor.

(2) Asset retention and utilisation pattern of IRDP assistance.

(3) Changes in income

(4) Crossing of poverty line.

(5) Loan recovery, and

(6) Implementational aspects, linkages and participation of IRDP beneficiaries.

The major findings of various studies coming under the above categories and other details are presented in Tables 2.1 to 2.6.

1. COVERAGE OF RURAL POOR

The main objective of IRDP is to increase the accessibility of rural poor to various institutional credit agencies by enlisting them under the programme. It may be seen from Table 2.1 that in almost all the studies,the bulk of the selected households come under the eligible category of rural poor. In other words, a significant proportion of the rural households assisted under IRDP are poor. Thus, it is possible to say from the Table that a large number of rural poor have been able to get institutional credit (assistance) by virtue of being selected under IRDP. At the same time, it may be seen that a considerable proportion of even the non-eligible or non-poor have also been able to get benefits under IRDP, though their proportion varies from study to study.

2. ASSET RETENTION AND UTILISATION PATTERN OF IRDP ASSISTANCE

Table 2.2 contains information about the extent of retention and sustainability of assets created under IRDP. The findings of the studies reveal that for a considerable proportion of households the assets have got decapitalised mid-way for various reasons. In such cases, the households have either diverted the assistance by selling the asset or the assets (animals) have died midway or have got decapitalised due to natural wear and tear over the years. Thus, though IRDP has been able to increase the asset holding of a large number of rural poor, the overall level of retention and sustainability of assets seems to be low.

3. CHANGES IN INCOME

The changes brought about in the income levels of the rural poor by IRDP as depicted by various studies are given in Table 2.3. Though there is an increase in the income levels of households coming under IRDP, the extent of change in income varies across different sectors and across households of different income groups. The proportion of income generated by IRDP to the pre-assistance income level varies for different households, but seems to be higher for households in the lower income group. The studies reveal that the income generated is higher for households pursuing activities in

Table 2.1 : Coverage of Rural Poor under IRDP

S. No.	Study Conducted by Scholar /s Agency	State	Study Area	Year	% age of Eligible Households
1.	Krishnan	Kerala	Calicut	1984	36
2.	PEO	—	—	1985	74
3.	Tripathy & Others	Orissa	Puri	1983	87
4.	The Central Bank of India	Madhya Pradesh	Chindwara	1983	72
5.	Centre for Development Studies	Kerala	Quilon	1983	79
6.	NABARD	Assam		1984	58
		Haryana		1984	82
		Punjab		1984	65
		Madhya Pradesh		1984	81
		Maharashtra		1984	87
		Tamil Nadu		1984	89
		Karnataka		1984	89
7.	Ahuja and Bhargava	Rajasthan	Jaipur	1984	85
8.	S. C. Jain	Gujarat	Surat	1984	90
9.	Canara Bank	Tamil Nadu	Tirunelveli & Periyar	1984	75
10.	Kartar Singh	—	—	1985	68
11.	B. Usha	Tamil Nadu	Ramanatha Puram	1984	91
12.	J. S. Sodhi	Maharastra	Satara	1987	74
		Rajasthan	Bhandara	1987	49
13.	Aranha and Kaundinya	Maharastra	Thane	1985	55
14.	Kerala Planning Board Survey	Kerala	—	1981	58
15.	D. Gianchandani et. al.	Northern & Eastern Rajasthan		1987	60
16.	N. J. Kurien	All-India	—	1987	80

Table 2.2 : Creation, Retention of Assets and Utilisation Pattern of IRDP Assistance

S. No.	Author/s Organisation	Year	Study Area	Major Findings of the Study
1.	Robert V Pulley	1989	Uttar Pradesh	The proportion of investments/ assets retention declined from 82 per cent after two years to 59% after 4 years.
2.	PEO	1985	—	Asset sold because of poor quality.
3.	Arul Annes	1988	—	50% of the assets sold belong to very very poor and very poor category of beneficiaries.
4.	K. V. Narayan et. al.	1989	Warangal (Andhra Pradesh)	By and large animals and other schemes availed were sold/ perished.
5.	N. J. Kurien	1987	All-India	1) 71% of assets are intact and the rest are not intact after 2 years of assistance. 2) The reasons for assets not intact are like unexpected event like death of family members/ illness or death of animal, high maintenance cost and defective assets.
6.	C. H. H. Rao & Rangaswamy	1988	Uttar Pradesh	On an average 20–30% of the assets across the different sectors are not intact.
7.	D. Gianchandani et. al.	1987	Northern & Eastern Rajasthan	1) Fake purchase of assets accounted for 24%. 2) Asset (Milch animals) sold to the tune of 14%. 3) Poor quality of assets under animal husbandary schemes was given.
8.	State Bank of Hyderabad	1983	Maharashtra Andhra Pradesh (Karnataka)	Misutilization of funds was about 32% in the case of animal husbandry schemes.
9.	C. H. Balaramulu	1988	Nalgonda (Andhra Pradesh)	IRDP assets were sold to meet the socio-economic needs of the beneficiaries.

Table 2.3 : Changes in Income and Output from IRDP Assets

S. No.	Author/s Organisation	Year	Study Area	Major Findings of the Study
1.	P. N. Mathur	1984	Maghalaya	IRDP (social forestry schemes in Meghalaya) beneficiaries income increased to the tune of 7%.
2.	K. Srinivasan	---	---	Fruit plantation scheme of IRDP increased yield in the case of small farms size class.
3.	State Bank of India	1987	—	The village and cottage industries schemes are most successful in income generation (Rs. 3,240) followed by agriculture sector (Rs. 2,259) territiary sector (Rs. 2,253).
4.	Robert L. Ayres	1985	—	IRDP beneficiaries have participated actively and milk yield has increased.
5.	B. Usha	1984	Ramanathapuram	1) Milk production and transaction in dairy cooperatives has increased. 2) Beneficiaries purchased land with the increased income generated by the milch animals.
6.	PEO	1985	—	88 per cent of the IRDP Househouseds reported that income has increased.
7.	B. Bowander et al.	1987	—	IRDP record evidence of benefit to the rural poor in terms of improvement in the income generation and food intake i.e., milk products, eggs etc.
8.	Kerala Planning Board Survey	1981	Kerala	For 31% of IRDP beneficiaries additional income generated by the asset is nil.
9.	M. C. Singh	---	Palamu (Bihar)	Assets generated low income because of tiny land holdings.
10.	S. Gadam	1986	Sangli Jalagaon (Maharashtra)	Incremental Capital Output Ratio (ICOR) was 4.9 as against the national average of 4.0.

Contd...

Table 2.3 : Contd.

S. No.	Author/s Organisation	Year	Study Area	Major Findings of the Study
11.	V. M. Gumaste et. al.	1987	Rajasthan West-Bengal, Orissa, Gujarat Karna-taka.	Income augmenting process has begun but still majority of the beneficiaries did not cross PL. The ICOR was 1.5 1 to that of the actual norm of 3:1.
12.	Govt. of India (Concurrent Evaluation Survey)	1985-86	All India	The percentage of incrementa income generated by the assets reported by the beneficiary of different income groups are as follows. 11% upto Rs. 500 15% from Rs. 501 to 1000, 24% from Rs. 1001 to Rs. 2000 and 26% more than Rs. 2000.
13.	Govt. of India (Concurrent Evaluation Survey)	Jan. 89 –June,89	All India	The additional income generated by the assets was more than Rs. 2000 in 27% of cases between Rs. 1000 and 2000 in 20% cases, Rs. 501 to 1000 in 12% of cases, and Rs. 500 in 35% cases of the assets did not gene-rate any income.
14.	Robert V. Pulley	1989	Uttar Pradesh	The ICOR for all the IRDP beneficiaries after 2 years and 4 years was 1.6 and 3, respect-vily.
15.	N. J. Kurian	1987	All India	50 per cent of the assets gene-rated income more than Rs. 1001. 11 per cent and 15 per cent of the assets income gene-ration was Rs. 1 to 500 and Rs. 501 to 1000, respectively. And 24 per cent of the assets did not generate income at all.
16.	C. H. H. Rao and Rangaswamy	1988	Uttar Pradesh	1) The ICOR for all schemes in UP was 1.66, the highest being 5.68 for borewell schemes and the lowest for tailoring (.71) and village industries (.94).

Contd...

Table 2.3 : Contd.

S. No.	Author/s Organisation	Year	Study Area	Major Findings of the Study
				2) The ICOR for primary sector was 2.66, secondary sector 1.06, and tertiary sector 1.31.
				3) The percentage of income increased by the IRDP assets was a little over 40% in the case of schemes under secondary and tertiary sectors. While primary sector schemes generated income increased to the tune of 21.4%. Overall net income increased by 33 per cent.
17.	Arul Annes	1988	----	The income generated by the schemes availed of by the very very poor was low and vice-versa in the case of others.

the tertiary and secondary sectors than those in the primary sector. Further,the studies also reveal two disquieting features of IRDP. First, a large number of assets have not been able to generate any income. Second, the overall productivity of investment-income generated by an unit of investment, as indicated by the Incremental Capital Output Ratio (ICOR) is also very low.

4. CROSSING OF POVERTY LINE

The main objective of credit-based poverty alleviation programmes like IRDP is to help the beneficiary households cross the poverty line through creation of income generating assets. How far IRDP has been able to achieve this objective is given by studies included in Table 2.4. The proportion of poor households crossing the poverty line varies from study to study. However, a careful perusal of the table shows that only a small proportion of the poor households has been able to cross the poverty line. Conversely,the studies reveal that given only a small increase in income, for majority of the households it has not been possible to move above the poverty line.

Table 2.4 : Crossing of Poverty Line

S. No.	Author/s Organisation	Year	Study Area	Major Findings of the Study
1.	K. Subba Rao	1985	All-India	Bottom group beneficiaries income has increased though they have not been able to cross poverty line (CPL).
2.	Govt. of India (Concurrent Evaluation Survey)	Jan.89 June 89	All-India	44% and 6% of the IRDP beneficiaries crossed PL of Rs.3,500 and Rs. 6,400, respectively.
3.	S. Gadam	1986	Sangli & Jalgaon (Maharashtra)	15% of the beneficiaries crossed PL.
4.	Rangaswami	1989	Rohtak (Haryana)	1) 2/3 of the beneficiaries who availed of the scheme under pretty shop crossed PL (Rs. 6400).
				2) ISB beneficiaries crossed PL more but most of their hereditary occupation coincides with the scheme.
5.	J. S. Sodhi	1985	Akola	42% CPL (Rs. 3,500).
		1987	Sawa Madhopur	40% CPL (Rs. 3,500)
		1987	Bhandara	24% CPL (Rs. 3,500)
6.	PED	1985	---	49.4% CPL (Rs. 3,500)
7.	NABARD	1984	---	47.1% CPL (Rs. 3,500).
8.	Ahuja and Bhargava	1985	Jaipur	23.2% CPL (Rs. 3,500).
9.	CDS	1983	Quilon	48.1% CPL (Rs. 3,500).
10.	Agarwal	1988	---	The percentage of people crossing poverty line ranged between 45 % and 50% in the case of allied activities and village and cottage industries, respectively.
11.	Thippaiah & D. Babu	1986	Dharward (Karnataka)	1) Income mobility seems to be more in the case of lower income groups than their counterparts.

Contd...

Table 2.4 : Contd.

S. No.	Author/s Organisation	Year	Study Area	Major Findings of the Study
				2) 31% of the beneficiaries moved above the poverty line (Rs. 3,500) of which 10.67 per cent were already above poverty line in the initial year itself.
12.	Institutional Finance and Statistics Deptt. (Govt. of Karnataka)	1985	Dharwad and Chikmagalur (Karnataka)	About 27.7 per cent of IRDP beneficiaries crossed poverty line.
13.	Govt. of India (Concurrent Evaluation Survey)	1985-86	All-India	52% and 12% of the beneficiaries crossed poverty line of Rs. 3,500 and Rs. 6,400 respectively.
		1986-87	All-India	60% and 13% of the beneficiaries crossed the poverty line of Rs. 3,500 and Rs. 6,400 respectively.
14.	Robert V. Pulley	1989	Uttar Pradesh	5% of the IRDP beneficiaries crossed poverty line (Rs. 6,400) after two years.
15.	S. Gadam	1986	Sangli & Jalgaon (Maharashtra)	6% of the households are above the PL initially, but came down below PL after availing of IRDP.
16.	Thimmaiah	1988	Karnataka	The IRDP schemes benefitted those who own land rather than those who do not i.e., agricultural labourers and those who have access to political power structure.
17.	C. H. H. Rao and Rangaswamy	1988	Uttar Pradesh	51% of the beneficiaries crossed the PL Rs. 3,500 and only 4.5% crossed the revised PL of Rs. 6,400.
18.	N. J. Kurien	1987	All-India	41% of IRD beneficiaries crossed PL of Rs. 3,500 in the country and only 5% crossed the revised PL of Rs. 6,400.

5. RECOVERY OF LOANS

The findings of available studies on repayment of loan borrowed under IRDP are presented in Table 2.5. The overall repayment of loans borrowed appears to be very low, though loans borrowed under the tertiary sector appear to be having relatively better repayment. The reasons for low recovery of loans vary from low productivity of investment to drought, absence of forward and backward linkages, mis-guidance on repayment, and rigid repayment schedule.

Table 2.5 : Loan Recovery Rate

S. No.	Author/s Organisation	Year	Study Area	Major Findings of the Study
1.	S. Gadam	1986	Sangli Jalagaon (Maharashtra)	Repayment of loans of all the schemes accounts for 82% (primary 89%, teritiary 74% and secondary 40%).
2.	K. V. Narayan et. al.	1986	Warangal (Andhra Pradesh)	1) Repayment seems to be negligible because of successive droughts in the region. 2) These mitigated further indebtedness to the beneficiaries.
3.	Malyadri	1988	Karim Nagar (Andhra Pradesh)	1) Repayment of loans accounted for 70%. 2) Non-repayment was attributed to high mortality rate of piglets and lack of forward and backward linkages.
4.	G. Thimmaiah	1988	Karnataka	Non-repayment of IRDP loans was attributed to the misguidance by the local political leaders.
5.	N. J. Kurien	1987	All-India	1) 45% of the beneficiaries do not have overdues. 2) Reasons for overdues are inadequate income generation by the assets (59%) unforeseen calamity (8%) rigid repayment schedule (30%) and others.
6.	C. H. H. Rao and Rangaswamy	1988	Uttar Pradesh	Schemes under the secondary sector record no overdues. While in the case of schemes sanctioned under the primary sector and tertiary sector the percentage of overdues to loans was 20.7 and 25.9 respectively, for all the sectors the figure was 22.9%.

6. IMPLEMENTATION, LINKAGES AND PARTICIPATION OF IRDP BENEFICIARIES

The findings of the studies dealing with the reasons for the success or failure of IRDP are given in Table 2.6. Almost all the studies reviewed deal with the reasons for failure of IRDP. The various reasons for the failure of IRDP to achieve its objective as revealed by the studies reviewed here are : absence of backward and forward linkages, fake transfer of assets to beneficiaries, failure to consider the skills of the beneficiaries, delay in delivery of schemes, frequent occurrence of droughts, lack of motivation and efficiency among the administrative staff, wrong identification of beneficiaries, over emphasis on agricultural schemes, lack of co-ordination among the implementing agencies and diversion of funds by middlemen. The studies reviewed thus attribute the failure of IRDP to many reasons emanating from various sources.

The above review of literature has attempted to reveal that a credit-based poverty alleviation programme like IRDP has been able to reach a large number of rural poor and thereby enabling them to acquire productive assets. However, a bulk of the households has not been able to sustain the activities taken up with IRDP assistance, as they have either misutilised the funds or the assets have got decapitalised for other reasons. Though the scheme could increase the overall incomes,particularly of the poor, the increase has neither been substantial nor sustainable. As a result, IRDP has not been able to achieve its main objective of alleviating rural poverty and lift the rural poor permanently above the poverty line.

Though the studies reviewed above have examined various issues connected with IRDP, they have not been able to analyse properly the socio-economic setting under which IRDP has been operating. At the same time, the role played by various institutions, particularly institutional credit agencies which play a crucial role in implementing programmes like IRDP, has not been brought out clearly. Not many studies, therefore, have attempted to study IRDP from a holistic angle. Besides, almost all studies have done only one- point evaluation of the scheme, which fails to bring out clearly the sustainability of the scheme as well as its impact.

Table 2.6 : Implementation, Linkages and Participation of IRDP Beneficiaries

S. No.	Author/s Organisation	Year	Study Area	Major Findings of the Study
1.	D. Sen & P. K. Das	1988	West Bengal	Napura Group Form Forestry Project in West Bengal was a success because of local industry, infrastructure base, encouragement of implementing agency etc.
2.	Indira Hirway	1983	—	Weak planning component in IRDP
		1984	Gujarat	IRDP failed due to lack of delivery of the package of inputs and services.
		1985	—	1) Transfer of asset take place only on paper.
		1985	—	2) Skills and option of the selection of the schemes by beneficiaries not considered.
3.	A. P. Saxena	1987	—	Delay in sanction/delivery of the schemes.
4.	A. R. Desai	1987	—	Bureaucratic way of implementing the IRDP.
5.	B. Kumar	1987	Sultanpur, Gonda, Bahraich dists. (U.P.)	1) Followed cluster approach in the beginning and dropped later on. 2) 35% of the beneficiaries felt that the asset value (purchased) was higher than the actual value prevailed.
6.	C. H. Balaramulu	1988	Nalgonda (A. P.)	1) Failure of IRDP Scheme because of droughts and floods. 2) Middle-men and untrained personnel involved in implementing the programme at grass root level.
7.	Robert V. Pulley	1989	Uttar Pradesh	The failure of IRDP was because of economic shocks like droughts and unable to make the rural poor to become creditworthy.

Table 2.6 : Contd.

S. No.	Author/s Organisation	Year	Study Area	Major Findings of the Study
8.	Rangaswamy	1989	Rohtak (Haryana)	Rural diversification seems to be dismal picture.
9.	N. Rath	1985	----	1) Proper integration has not been done either spatially or at sectoral, block level to improve the levels of living of IRDP beneficiaries.
10.	M. Gopinath Reddy	1989	East Godavari (Andhra Pradesh)	1) Lack of motivation, promotional avenues and interest on fringe benefits among the block level staff. 2) Inadequate block level staff to implement IRDP. 3) Lack of autonomy to the block level staff 4) Lack of coordination (horizontal and vertical) of implementing agency.
11.	V. M. Gumaste et. al.	1987	Rajasthan West Bengal Orissa Gujarat Karnataka	1) Misidentification of beneficiaries, over emphasis on agricultural schemes and dairy. 2) Level of investment on IRDP beneficiaries was not co-inciding with level of development of the region. 3) Lack of coordination by the implementing agency.
12.	G. Rami Reddy & G. Hara Gopal	1984	----	Cumbersome rules and regulations and also middlemen role was more.
13.	M. Shivashankaraih & P. Ramappa	1989	Anantapur (Andhra Pradesh)	1) Lack of qualitative and timely supply of feeds and poultry birds, lack of co-ordination by the implementing agency, storage problem (for both eggs and feeds), inadequate/lack of training to IRDP beneficiaries and finally the IRDP poultry units were closed.

Contd...

Table 2.6 : Contd.

S. No.	Author/s Organisation	Year	Study Area	Major Findings of the Study
				2) Mortality rate of poultry birds sponsored under IRDP was high as compared to the private poultry units in the study area.
14.	Ministry of Agri. and Rural Development, Govt. of India.	1985	----	Lack of inter-sectoral connectivity.
15.	Mukul Sanwal	1985	-----	Lack of forward and backward linkages
16.	K. V. Narayana et. al.	1986	Warangal (Andhra Pradesh)	Inadequate veterinary services and low demand for bullock and bullock carts in the study area.
17.	Abdul Aziz	1987	Kolar Dharwad (Karnataka)	1. Integration of block resources and sectoral plans seems to be marginal initiation by DRDA, DIC and other departments in the study districts. Household plan had not been integrated between the above factors.
18.	Institutional Finance and Statistics Deptt. (Govt. of Karnataka)	1985	Dharwad Chikmangalur (Karnataka)	1) Block plans were not prepared either at district level or by the concerned banks. 2) Administrative expenditure exceeds 7.5 per cent of the total expenditure which is more than the norm/guidelines of IRDP.
19.	Govt. of India (Concurrent Evaluation Survey)	1985-86	All-India	85% of the beneficiaries reported favourable availability of inputs and marketing facilities
20.	Govt. of India (Concurrent Evaluation Survey)	1989-89 (Jan.– June)	All-India	The inputs and marketing of the product are inadequate after IRDP assistance.
21.	N. J. Kurien	1987	All-India	55%, 4% and 5% of the beneficiaries were identified by grama sabha, officials and others, respectively.
22.	H. Escher	1986	Hingangaon (Maharashtra)	Dairy schemes of those who had availed of under IRDP formed milk cooperative society at Hingangaon, Maharashtra.

3

Objectives and Methodology

OBJECTIVES OF THE STUDY

Keeping the various issues raised with regard to poverty in general and IRDP in particular in the previous two chapters, the following objectives have been formulated for the present study:-

1. To assess the role of state intervention in alleviating rural poverty in Karnataka.
2. To analyse the impact of IRDP on socio-economic conditions of the beneficiaries.
3. To examine the role of Financial institutions like Commercial Banks (CBs) and Regional Rural Banks (RRBs) in implementing IRDP.
4. To examine various policy alternatives for better implementation of poverty alleviation programmes.

METHODOLOGY

The methodology followed in this study is discussed below :

Data Base

This study is based on both secondary and primary sources of data. The secondary data is collected from various annual reports, published and unpublished documents of the rural development department and plan documents. The information collected from these reports relates to a number of on-going anti-poverty programmes, physical and financial achievements of IRDP since its inception, coverage of beneficiaries by type and by schemes. The purpose here is to understand the implementation of anti-poverty programmes at a macro-level i.e., at the State level.

The primary data for the study is collected from the Concurrent Evaluation Survey (CES) of IRDP conducted by the Institute for Social and Economic Change (ISEC), Bangalore. ISEC,along with other research organisations, participated in the first round of country-wide Concurrent Evaluation of IRDP conducted between October 1985 and September 1986. The ISEC survey which covered 20 blocks in ten districts in Karnataka, was entrusted by the Ministry of Agriculture and Rural Development, Government of India. The total number of IRDP beneficiaries covered in the survey was 390. The CES data was supplemented by data collected through this researcher's own interview schedules from sample beneficiaries.

The main reason for using the Concurrent Evaluation data lies in the fact that the author of this study had participated in all the stages of the survey as a member of the team.

Selection of the Study Area

The following methodology was used by the CES for the selection of the sample households. Firs , a list of the IRDP beneficiaries assisted in each block by cluster and also by villages was prepared. The cluster was selected based on the village where the highest number of IRDP beneficiaries were assisted. Then, that village which came under a particular cluster was selected in the first instance. The second village selection should represent similar (to that of the first village) agro-climatic condition or nearby village within a radius of 5 km.

In each of the 10 districts surveyed, two blocks were covered and in each block, four-villages (two villages each representing 'current' beneficiaries and 'old' beneficiaries) were selected. The 'current' beneficiaries are those who have received the IRDP scheme within three months prior to the date of the CES visit and 'old' beneficiaries were those who had availed of the assistance 24 to 27 months prior to the visit. In each block 10 'current' and 10 'old' (5 beneficiaries in each village) beneficiaries were selected. In one of the blocks, there were no 'current' beneficiaries and hence, the total number of beneficiaries contacted came to 390 (200 'old' and 190 'current').

The IRDP beneficiaries (both 'current' and 'old') were selected from the list which was available in the BDO's office by using the simple random sampling method. The details about distribution of sample beneficiaries by districts, blocks and villages is given in Table 3.1.

The following procedures were followed to collect the information for this study. The information pertaining to IRDP beneficiaries was collected from District Rural Development Agency (DRDA) or Block Development Offices (BDOs) in the study area. Interview technique was adopted to collect appropriate information from the IRDP beneficiaries with the help of an interview schedule. Three types of schedules were canvassed apart from CES schedule, namely,Village Schedule, Household Schedule and Bank Schedule to gather information about the type/structure of the villages, details about the respondents (other than IRDP particulars), exact position on the loan particulars and repayment, respectively.

The details of the interview schedules prepared and canvassed by the researcher are indicated in the following paragraphs:-

(1) **Village Schedule** : The items which are covered in this schedule are broadly categorised as infrastructure facilities, educational institutions, caste composition, cropping pattern, beneficiary organisations, experience of droughts in the past years and the ongoing development programmes to ease out drought effect (particularly to the target group) in the selected villages. The above information was collected from the local Panchayat Office and also through discussion with the elders in the concerned villages. All these variables were expected to help in assessing the strength of the economic base of the village.

(2) The Household Schedule : Two types of household schedules were canvassed. The first schedule was used to collect details of household information. This included particulars like land holdings, type of occupation, cropping pattern and the crop yield, cattle population, consumer durables owned and purchased within 5 years, type of houses, food habits, use of electricity, demographic

Table 3.1 : Distribution of Sample Households by Districts, Blocks and Villages

District	Block	No. of Clusters	Villages	No. of Beneficiaries covered under IRDP	No. of Beneficiaries selected
BIDAR	A. Basavakalyan	12	1. Kinni	15	5
			2. Kherda (B)	21	5
	B. Bidar	15	1. Chikpeth	17	5
			2. Benakanalli	35	5
	C. Gulbarga	23	1. Nandur (B)	69	5
			2. Dharmapur	72	5
GULBARGA	D. Sedum	11	1. Yadhalli	59	5
			2. Habal T	21	5
	E. B. Bagewadi	7	1. Ingaleshwar	14	5
			2. Masabinal	31	5
BIJAPUR	F. Bilgi	9	1. Mannikeri	7	5
			2. Girisagar	10	5
	G. Hukkeri	6	1. Bellambi	26	5
			2. Shellapur	8	5
BELGAUM	H. Khanapur	8	1. Kerwad (Gundenatti)	18	5
			2. Linganmath	9	5
	I. Hangal	8	1. Kondoji	23	5
			2. Shedguppi	42	5
DHARWAD	J. Haveri	7	1. Chikkalin-gadahalli	54	5
			2. Hommardi	12	5
	K. Jagalur	8	1. Urlakatte	14	5
			2. Pallakatte	39	5
CHITRA-DURGA	L. Challakere	11	1. Ghataparthi	33	5
			2. Chtranaikanahalli	15	5
	M. Sringeri	7	1. Vykuntapur	8	5
			2. Kochavalli	5	5
CHIKMA-GALUR	N. Mudigere	9	1. Mudigere (R)	38	5
			2. Lokavalli	18	5

Contd.

Table 3.1 : Contd.

District	Block	No. of Clu-sters	Villages	No. of Bene-ficiaries covered under IRDP	No. of Bene-ficiaries sele-cted
	O. Manjarabad (Shaklespur)	6	1. Kyamanahalli	11	5
			2. Byakarahalli	21	5
HASSAN					
	P. Channarayapatna	12	1. Kalenahalli	26	5
			2. Bediganahalli	34	5
	Q. Somwarpet	6	1. Thakery	26	5
			2. Kirganduru	36	5
KODAGU	R. Virajpet	8	1. Kottoli	83	5
			2. Kedamullur	58	5
	S. Nelamangala	6	1. Thippasettihalli	7	5
			2. Karehalli	6	5
BANGA-LORE (Rural)	T. Hoskote	6	1. Sonnalipura	9	5
			2. Kambalipura	14	5

details and other sources of income. This information was collected to understand the households' socio-economic background. The second schedule prepared by the Ministry dealt mainly with various IRDP particulars of the households.

(3) A Brief Schedule on Bank Data : This was designed and canvassed to gather information on IRDP beneficiaries about the loan amount, interest rate, subsidy amount, number of repayment instalments, repayment made, overdues position and any other loans sanctioned to the same household. The purpose of this schedule is to know the transactions taking place between the beneficiary households and the banks.

Method of Analysis

The methodology followed in the analysis of the study is as follows :-

First, a brief descriptive account of the anti-poverty programmes implemented in Karnataka in general and a detailed analysis of IRDP in particular is examined. This includes the IRDP's physical and financial achievements and coverage of SC/STs, women and Industries, Services and Business (ISB) beneficiaries by districts and for the State.

The 20 development blocks under which these sample households fall are classified broadly as, Developed Blocks and Backward Blocks, based on a study (Hemalatha Rao : 1984). Accordingly, out of 20 there were 6 relatively developed and 14 relatively backward blocks. The blocks are classified on the basis of the development scores* (Table 3.2). Those development blocks having positive development scores are called developed blocks and those having negative scores backward blocks. Further, the blocks have been grouped into four different agro-climatic zones viz., North Dry Zone (NDZ), South Dry Zone (SDZ), Transition Zone (TZ) and Plantation Zone (PZ). The main purpose of classifying blocks into developed and backward blocks and also their grouping into agro-climatic zones is to see the pattern of IRDP performance across different regions. Also to find out whether such delineation has any impact on the level of participation of the beneficiaries by regions and by different schemes.

The sample beneficiaries have also been classified into three economic status categories viz., upper, middle, bottom, (Rao and Erappa : 1987). The purpose of this classification is to understand how the poor across different categories have performed under IRDP. When a programme like IRDP is implemented, it is necessary to know the type of households which can absorb the programme in terms of their level of perception about the utility and sustainability

---

The development scores are assigned by Hemalatha Rao in her study (1984) for each block in Karnataka. The following indicators were considered for arriving at the development scores:-

1. Agricultural Development Index
2. General Industrial Development Index
3. Small Scale Industrial Development Index
4. Educational Development Index
5. Health Development Index
6. Transport Index
7. Communication Development Index
8. Banking Development Index
9. Co-operative Sectoral Development Index
10. Power Development Index.

Table 3.2 : Ranking of Blocks by Development Score

S. No.	Name of the Block/ District	Development Score	Agro-Climatic Zone
1.	Hosakote (Bangalore)	11	South Dry Zone (SDZ)
2.	Virajpet Coorg)	7	Plantation Zone (PZ)
3.	Somwarpet (Coorg)	4	Plantation Zone
4.	Bidar (Bidar)	3	Transition Zone (TZ)
5.	Sringeri (Chickmagalur)	2	Plantation Zone
6.	Sakeleshpur (Hassan)	1	Plantation Zone
7.	Gulbarga (Gulbarga)	0	North Dry Zone (NDZ)
8.	Haveri (Dharwad)	–2	North Dry Zone
9.	Hukkeri (Belgaum)	–3	North Dry Zone
10.	Mudigere (Chickmagalur)	–4	Plantation Zone
11.	Nelamangala (Bangalore)	–4	South Dry Zone
12.	Hangal (Dharwad)	–5	Transition Zone
13.	Channarayapatna (Hassan)	–6	South Dry Zone
14.	Challakere (Chitradurga)	–7	South Dry Zone
15.	Jagalur (Chitradurga)	–7	South Dry Zone
16.	Khanapur (Belgaum)	–9	Transition Zone
17.	Biligi (Bijapur)	–10	North Dry Zone
18.	Basava Kalyana (Bidar)	–11	Transition Zone
19.	Sedam (Gulbarga)	–11	North Dry Zone
20.	Basavana Bagewadi (Bijapur)	–11	North Dry Zone

Source: Hamalatha Rao (1989) Regional Disparities and Development in India, Ashish Publishing House, New Delhi, pp. 302–316.

of the programme in the long run. The method followed in the classification of beneficiary households into three economic status groups is as follows:-

The households in the **upper** group :
a) Having a pucca house
b) Uses electricity in the house
c) At least one child in the age group of 5-15 attending school

d) Possesses conspicious consumer durables

The households that come under **bottom** group are :

a) Landless labourers the (neither owning nor cultivating)
b) At least one wage earner in the household in the age group of 5-15.

The households which do not come under the above two categories were classified as those belonging to the **middle** economic status category.

The impact of IRDP is analysed descriptively, by comparing the annual family income of the beneficiary household before and after the scheme. The analysis of impact of IRDP on beneficiaries is examined across social groups, women beneficiaries, different types of development blocks and various agro-climatic conditions. To examine the socio-economic impact of IRDP, income generated by the schemes has been analysed. In addition to this Incremental Capital Output Ratio (ICOR) and income mobility have also been analysed to measure the impact of IRDP. Further, the distribution of schemes and the acceptance level of the schemes by economic categories, status of the block and agro-climatic zones, the repayment made and the number of beneficiaries crossing the official poverty line have been analysed.

To study the role of financial institutions in implementing IRDP, the Commercial Banks (CBs) and Regional Rural Banks (RRBs) which are participating in implementing IRDP have been considered. Here details such as extra cost incurred by the beneficiaries to get the loans sanctioned, number of days spent to get loan and types of schemes sanctioned by these institutions have also been analysed.

Revisits

Between the time of assistance (1983-84) and the writing of the thesis (1990-91), there was a gap of nearly 7 years. During this period it is possible that many changes would have taken place not only in the socio-economic conditions of the beneficiaries but also in their perceptions to the problem of poverty and poverty alleviation programmes. Also, with the lapse of time the issue of sustainability of the poverty alleviation schemes and their benefits also become important. Hence, the need was felt for updating the information on socio-economic dynamics of the beneficiaries households. It was, therefore, decided to conduct a revisit to the beneficiary households to collect information on the changes that have occurred in their socio-economic conditions and in their perceptions.

Since it was not possible to cover all the 200 beneficiaries interviewed during the CES, it was decided to contact 40 beneficiaries for the purpose in 8 villages representing different development blocks. The revisits were conducted in two developed blocks and two backward blocks. The revisited blocks, villages and beneficiaries are drawn from old beneficiaries of the CES. The villages which come under the above two types of blocks also represent the four agro-climatic zones. The details of the revisited zones, blocks, villages and IRDP beneficiaries are given in Table 3.3.

Table 3.3 : Revisited Zones, Blocks, Villages and IRDP Beneficiaries during 1990-91

Zones	Block	Status of the Block	Villages	No. of IRDP Beneficiaries
SDZ	Hosakote	Developed	A. Sonallipura	5
			B. Kamblipura	5
NDZ	Haveri	Backward	A. Chikkalingadahalli	5
			B. Hombardi	5
TZ	Hangal	Backward	A. Shydaguppi	5
			B. Kondoji	5
PZ	Sringeri	Developed	A. Vykuntapura	5
			B. Kochavalli	5

At the time of revisits, apart from canvassing a brief structured interview schedule, discussions were held with the individual beneficiaries, bank officials and elders (other than IRDP beneficiaries in those villages). Further the implementation of the Agricultural Debt Relief Scheme* (ADRS) during 1990 by the concerned financial institutions was also taken into account.

* Agricultural Debt Relief Scheme initiated by the Central Government to the chronic overdues (particularly IRDP) to waive off the maximum relief amount of Rs. 10,000 between the period of 2.10.86 and 2.10.89. The criteria followed to sanction ADRS to IRDP beneficiaries are (i) The village should be declared as *Annewari* (for details see Chapter 7). (ii) The IRDP beneficiaries should be declared insolvent in the court (iii) IRDP beneficiary should have expired, and (iv) The overdues that fall between 2.10.86 and 2.10.89 to be eligible for ADRS.

The data collected during revisits include, among other things, particulars of loan repayment, any supplementary assistance to the beneficiaries, the actual amount of assistance got through ADRS, the status of the loan and changes occurred at the beneficiary households.

Based on the data collected during revisits, an attempt has been made to examine the IRDP beneficiary perception, their absorption capabilities of the scheme, the level of transformation that has taken place at the households in terms of sustainability, income mobility, improvement in literacy rate (children) and the enhancement of socio-economic conditions. Case studies of a few beneficiaries also has been attempted.

Limitations of the Study

This study has some limitations. While primary data is collected from the respondents, particularly on income, to assess the economic impact of IRDP loans subject to the problem of memory recall. Since this study covers 10 districts of Karnataka, the findings of the study may not give the total picture of the state. Further, while selecting the samples from the list of the IRDP beneficiaries made available by the BDO office, due weightage has not been given to different schemes and sectors.

Organisation of the Study

The organisation of the chapter scheme of this study is indicated in the following paragraphs:-

General introduction on poverty, statement of the problem, the conceptual issues on poverty, Third World nations' (including that of India) experiences on poverty alleviation are discussed in Chapter 1.

In Chapter 2, a review of the literature on poverty is presented in two parts. Part I gives a historical view starting from Mercantalist to Development economists. A few theories on poverty, probably, provide different facets of rural poverty and its eradication. Further, under what conditions is rural poverty perpetuating and who are the people suffering from this, are also discussed in this chapter.

Continuing Chapter 2, a review of literature on the Integrated Rural Devleopment Programme (IRDP), studies highlighting its various dimensions in understanding the problem of rural poverty by individual scholar/s, organisations and their suggestion are discussed in Part II. The studies on IRDP were broadly classified under different heads. While doing so, an attempt is made to identify the research gaps.

The objective and methodology of this study are spelt out in the present 3 chapter.

In Chapter 4, a brief outline ot the anit-poverty programmes in general and IRDP in particular, implemented in Karnataka with studies and estimations of the incidence of poverty available is presented. Furthermore, the details of the study area and the profile of the blocks/villages by selected indicators and socio-economic-demographic characteristics of IRDP beneficiaries are discussed.

In Chapter 5, a detailed analysis of the data on IRDP beneficiaries based on their social groups and the schemes, women beneficiaries coverage, performance of IRDP beneficiaries in different development blocks and also in agro-climatic zones and related issues are discussed.

In Chapter 6, the role of financial institutions and poverty alleviation programmes in Karnataka is presented. Furhter, a comparative analysis of the performance of CBs and RRBs in implementing IRDP is also highlighted in this Chapter.

In Chapter 7, the analysis based on revisits made to a few beneficiaries (whom we met at the time of the concurrent evaluation survey) covering four agro-climatic zones during 1990-91 is presented. A few case studies (the success or failure) of IRDP beneficiaries are also presented in this Chapter.

In Chapter 8, we present the summary and conclusions of the study. Based on the analysis and inferences appropriate policy implications are drawn to alleviate rural poverty at the end.

4

Anti-Poverty Programmes in India

The main focus of this chapter is to look at the poverty situation in Karnataka and prepare an inventory of various anti-poverty programmes before analysing their impact. This chapter contains three sections. The first section outlines the geographical and economic characteristics of Karnataka. The second section presents the details about the anti-poverty programmes being implemented in Karnataka. The third section draws a profile of the selected blocks, villages and IRDP beneficiaries.

I

A BRIEF PROFILE OF KARNATAKA (A CASE STUDY)

Karnataka is rich in natural resources and has a wide range of agro-climatic conditions. The reorganised Karnataka State came into being in 1956. The State is located in the western part of the Deccan Plateau in the country. It is located between 11°31' and 18°45' North latitudes and 74°12' and 78°40' East longitudes (Karnataka Gazetteer : 1982, p.5). The climate of the State is tropical in nature with an annual (normal) average rainfall of 1139 mm during 1957-1990 (Directorate of Economics and Statistics : 1991).

The geographical area of the State is 1.92 lakh sq.km. with a population of 44.8 millions in 1991. The density of population was 238 persons pr sq.km., which is less than the national average of 267 in 1991. The sex ratio is 963 which is above the all-India figure of 933. The decennial population growth rate between 1981 and 1991 was 20.67 per cent in the State. The Scheduled Caste population accounted for 15.1 per cent and Scheduled Tribes for 4.9 per cent of the total population in the State (Census of India : 1981 cited in Inter State Economic Indicator, p.8). The percentage of Effective Literacy Rate (ELR) of Karnataka in 1991 was 55.98 per cent. The ELR for male and female was 67.25 per cent and 44.34 per cent, respectively

The per capita income of the State has increased from Rs.1,454 in 1978-79 to Rs.4,305 in 1989-90 at current prices (Planning Department, Government of Karnataka, Economic Survey : 1991-92, p.12). The foodgrain production in Karnataka during the period 1989-90 was 70.58 lakh tonnes (Ibid, Appendix 2.3, p.A-3). The percentage of main workers to total population has increased from 34.74 per cent in 1971 to 36.76 per cent in 1981 in the State (Government of Karnataka, perspective plan 2001 : 1988, Table 3, p.22c). The cultivators and agricultural labourers account for 38.25 per cent and 26.78 per cent of working population in 1981, respectively.

The composition of population by religion in Karnataka shows that Hindus account for 86 per cent, Muslims, 11 per cent, the rest being accounted for by Christians, Buddhists and Jains in 1981 (Census of India : 1981). The Infrastructure Development Index (IDI) 1986-87 of Karnataka State (100), though tallying with the national average (100), is far below the level of Punjab (216), Haryana (149), Tamil Nadu (142) and Kerala (140) (CMIE : 1988).

The number of Fair Price Shops (FPS) increased from 14,227 in 1982 to 16,427 in 1987. The population served per FPS was higher (2,569) in Karnataka than for all-India (2,293)in 1987 (Directorate of Economies and Statistics, Government of India : 1985).

The composition of rural workers in Karnataka by sex in 1981 and 1991 is given in Table 4.1. The percentage of cultivators (both male and female) to total cultivators, which was 47.81 per cent in 1981 has decreased to 43.99 per cent, while the proportion of

Table 4.1 : Composition of Rural Workers in 1981 and 1991 in Karnataka

(in percentage)

Item	1981			1991		
	Male	*Female*	*Total*	*Male*	*Female*	*Total*
1. Cultivators	55.32	28.36	47.81	50.83	30.04	43.99
2. Agricultural Labourers	23.63	55.04	32.37	26.22	55.09	35.71
3. Household Industry	2.82	5.32	3.53	2.48	2.09	2.35
4. Other Workers	18.23	11.28	16.29	20.47	12.78	17.95
Total	**100.00**	**100.00**	**100.00**	**100.00**	**100.00**	**100.00**

Source: Census of India 1991, Provisional Population Totals, Workers and their Distribution, paper-3 of 1991, Series-1, Registrar General and Census Commissioner of India, New Delhi, p. 433-435.

agricultural labourers has increased from 32.4 per cent to 35.7 per cent during the same period. The percentage of rural workers under household industry has declined by about 1 per cent. The other workers category shows an increase of about 1 per cent. The proportion of female labour as compared to male category in all activities shows an increase,except in the household industry during the period.

The cropped area accounted for 61 per cent of the geographical area of the State,as per village holding across different sizes is given in Table 4.2. The number of holdings and area operated under small and marginal size class have increased between 1976-77 to 1985-86 in the State.

The area declared as surplus land under the revised land ceiling laws as on March 1983 was 2.96 lakh acres, but the area distributed was only 1.05 lakh acres. Out of the total beneficiaries of 24,400 in the State, SC & STs constitute 15.6 per cent and 2.5 per cent, respectively (Report of the Commissioner for SC/STs: 1982-83). The number of bonded labourers identified and freed accounted for 42,689 and those rehabilitated accounted for 40,033 as on March 1986 in the state. The minimum wages for agricultural operation for unskilled labourers range from Rs.9.50 to Rs.14 per day, as on 20th May 1987, in the State (CMIE: 1988).

Table 4.2 : Distribution of Land Holdings Pattern in Karnataka

(in lakh hectare)

Size Class (ha.)	1976-77			1985-86			1990-91		
	No. of holdings	Operated area	Average holdings size	No. of holdings	Area	Average holding size	No. of holdings	Area	Average holding size
Below 1	12.74 (33)	6.38 (6)	0.50	17.88 (37)	8.66 (7)	0.48	22.62 (39)	10.72 (9)	0.48
1 – 2	8.88 (23)	13.19 (11)	1.49	12.83 (26)	18.86 (16)	1.47	15.86 (28)	23.06 (19)	1.46
2 – 4	8.18 (22)	22.87 (20)	2.80	10.33 (21)	28.78 (24)	2.79	11.63 (20)	32.00 (26)	2.76
4 – 10	6.31 (17)	38.58 (34)	6.11	6.45 (13)	38.81 (33)	6.02	6.36 (11)	37.70 (30)	5.93
10 +	1.99 (5)	32.54 (29)	16.30	1.53 (3)	23.65 (20)	15.46	1.29 (2)	19.71 (16)	15.28
Total	**38.10 (100)**	**113.56 (100)**	**2.98**	**49.02 (100)**	**118.78 (100)**	**2.42**	**57.76 (100)**	**123.21 (100)**	**2.14**

Note : Figures in brackets are to total.

Source : a) Agricultural Census in India 1976-77 and for 1985-86.

b) Report on Census of Agricultural Holdings in Karnataka Part II, State Agricultural Census Commission, Bangalore 1990, Tables 2.1 and 2.2.

c) Agricultural Census 1990-01 Provisional Results, State Agricultural Census Commissioner, Government of Karnataka, Bangalore, Table 1, P7.

POVERTY ESTIMATIONS IN KARNATAKA

A brief account of the incidence of poverty is presented to highlight the magnitude of poverty in Karnataka. The following paragraphs give an account of various studies undertaken on this subject in the state.

The estimation of region-wise incidence of rural poverty in Karnataka was made by Sen Gupta and Joshi for 1972-73. The incidence of poverty was very high in Inland Northern districts as compared to the Southern districts in the state (Table 4.3). The coastal regions also show a higher incidence poverty as compared to the other regions.

Table 4.3 : Region-wise Incidence of Rural Poverty for 73 in Karnataka

S. No.	Region/State	Rural	
		Poverty Line (Rs.)	% of Population Below Poverty Line
1.	Coastal Ghats	52.57	76.32
2.	Inland Eastern	42.62	54.74
3.	Inland Southern	40.00	44.45
4.	Inland Northern	64.20	82.21
	Karnataka	**41.34**	**54.35**

Source: S. Sen Gupta and P. D. Joshi (1989).

The rural poor constitutes 35.0 per cent of the population during 1983-84 in the State. The percentage of rural poor to the total poor accounted for about 75 per cent in Karnataka, which is less than the national average of 81.73 per cent (Sinha : 1989). Table 4.4 gives the details of es.imates made by different researchers to show the percentage of the population living below the poverty line in Karnataka. According to Sen Gupta and Joshi (1989), the poverty ratio was 54 per cent at Rs.41.34 level during 1972-73 in rural Karnataka.

As per Datta's (1979) study, the incidence of rural poverty reached the peak during 1970 and declined thereafter, both at the State level and also at the national level. He has assumed the fixed expenditure of Rs.49.09 to be sufficient to meet the calorie requirement of 2,400 in rural areas.

P. J. Nayak and Sumithra (1985) estimated that the proportion of rural poor in Karnataka was 73.2 per cent and at all-India level it was 67 per cent, based on 1983 NSS (38 round) data. By using the same data, the Government of Karnataka in its Seventh Plan estimated that the proportion of people below the poverty line was 61 per cent. The higher estimation made by Nayak and Sumitra was attributed mainly to the inclusion of protein adequacy

Table 4.4 : Percentage of Population (Rural) Below Poverty Line in Karnataka and India

(Estimates)

S. No.	Individuals/ Organisations	Reference Year	Rural	
			Karnataka	All-India
1.	Datta (1989)			
	a. NSS case	1973-74	58.20	55.50
	b. CSO case	1973-74	50.60	47.60
2.	Sinha (189)	1983-84	35.00	37.40
3.	Sen Gupta and Joshi (1989)	1972-73	54.35	52.51
4.	Planning Commission (Seventh Plan)	1977-78	50.80	48.30
5.	Planning Commission (Seventh Plan)	1983-84	35.00	37.40
6.	Thimmaiah	1974-75	30.65	NA
7.	Seventh Five Year Plan, Govt. of Karnataka Poverty Index	1983	61.00	NA
8.	P. J. Nayak & Sumithra	1983	73.2	67.00
9.	Bardhan (1986)	1974.75	37.07	NA
10.	B. S. Minhas et. al. (1991) Head Count Ratio	1970-71	52.82	58.75
		1983	40.26	50.77
		1987-88	42.26	48.69

Source : Compiled from the above studies.

as an indicator of nourishment. Ahluwalia (1978) established an evidence of a significant negative relationship between agricultural output per head and the incidence of poverty in rural Karnataka through trend values of agricultural production and rural poverty. M. H. Suraya Narayana (1983) found that there was no real improvement in the living condition of the rural poor in Karnataka since 1961-62 to 1973-74. The percentage of population below the poverty line (Rs. 3,500) was 48.3 per cent during 1977-78 and was reduced to 35.0 per cent in 1983-84 in Karnataka (CMIE : 1988).

Vijay Naik and Shailaja Prasad (1984) attempted to estimate the percentage of SC/ST and non-SC/ST population below the poverty line, based on consumption expenditure (at Rs. 49.09

poverty line) for rural Karnataka. The study reveals that 80 per cent of the SC/STs and 59 per cent of the non-SC/STs were below the poverty line during 1973-74.

Thimmaiah's (1982) study makes an attempt to estimate the incidence of poverty at disaggregated levels in Karnataka and it concludes that: (a) poverty is inversely associated with levels of development of the district (b) poverty is very high among muslims, SC/STs and other backward classes (c) poverty is very high among illiterates, agricultural labourers and small and marginal farmers.

FIVE-YEAR PLANS AND ANTI-POVERTY PROGRAMMES IN KARNATAKA

Initially, the anti-poverty programmes were classified under the heads of Social Servies and Community Development/Rural Development & Cooperation for allocating funds. Table 4.5 indicates the allocations made for social services and rural development during Five Year Plans and Annual Plans. The allocation was very marginal in the early plan periods and has increased steadily since the Fifth Five Year Plan.

The percentage of allocation of funds for anti-poverty programmes, includes the minimum needs programmes, to the total budget during the Sixth and Seventh Plans was 17 per cent and 20 per cent respectively in Karnataka. Table 4.6 gives the details of financial expenditure and physical achievements during the Seventh Plan. Obviously, the expenditure on wage employment programmes was more than on other rural development programmes in Karnataka. Next to wage employment programmes, expenditure on IRDP was higher, with an allocation of Rs. 129.11 crores and generation of 6.84 lakhs man-days in the State (Table 4.6).

Table 4.6a indicate the details of targets and physical achievements of Rural Development Programmes in Karnataka. The physical achievements to the targets under IRDP and 100 well programme was quite encouraging as compared to other Rural Development Programme in the early Eight Plan Period.

PERFORMANCE OF ANTI-POVERTY PROGRAMMES IN KARNATAKA

The various anti-poverty programmes being implemented in Karnataka may be grouped under eight broad categories viz., Asset creating schemes, employment generating programmes, skill for-

Table 4.5 : Plan Outlays and Allocations under Social Services and Rural Development in Karnataka

Plan	Total Outlay (Rs. in crores)	Social Services as % of total outlay	Community Development, Rural Development cooperation as % of total outlay
First Plan	48	8	4
Second Plan	145	22	9
Third Plan	250	20	9
Annual Plan			
1966-67	53	14	6
1967-68	60	12	4
1968-69	51	15	4
Fourth Plan	300	13	4
Fifth Plan	1350	24	4
Sixth Plan	2771	17	4
Seventh Plan	4768	21	4
Annual Plan			
1990-91	1302	24	7
1991-92	1774	24	6
Eighth Plan	12300	26	4
1992-93	2033	25	5

Source : Compiled from Plan Documents.

mation programmes, area development programmes, special programmes for weaker sections, welfare programmes, minimum needs programmes and other programmes. Each category aims at achieving a definite objective to help the weaker sections. In all, there are about 40 programmes currently being implemented in the State. Some of them are sponsored by the Central Government and quite a few by the State Government. Among the anti-poverty programmes, allocation of funds to wage employment programmes viz., NREP, RLEGP (Now merged and called Jawahar Rojgar Yojana) is higher, followed by IRDP. The Wage employment programmes aim at creating employment opportunities to rural poor, mainly during the slack agricultural season and also try to

Table 4.6 : Expenditure on Important Rural Development and Panchayat Raj Programmes in Seventh Plan (1985-90) and Physical Achievements in Karnataka

Programme	Seventh Plan 1985–90		
	Financial Expenditure (Rs. lakhs)	Physical Achievements	
		Units	Nos.
1. National Rural Employment Programme	14,933	Lakh Mandays	731
2. Rural Landless Employment Guarantee Programme	11,668	,,	811
3. Jawahar Rojgar Yojana	10,943	,,	408
4. Rural Employment Guarantee Scheme	748	NA	NA
5. Drought-prone Area Programme	5160	NA	NA
6. Western Ghat Development Programme	3,446	NA	NA
7. Integrated Rural Development Programme	12,911	Lakh Mandays	6.84
8. 100 Well Programme	2,267	Lakh Nos.	.63
9. Assistance of Surplus Land Grantees	286	Nos.	11,440
10. Development of Women and Children in Rural Areas	155	No. of groups	1,100
11 Anthyodaya	667	Lakh Nos.	46

Source: Draft Eighth Five Year Plan 1992-97, Planning Department, Government of Karnataka, December 1991, Compiled from Tables 1 and 2, p. VIII-3.

create infrastructural base in the rural areas. These programmes basically act as some sort of a relief-oriented programme to the rural poor.

In other words, wage employment programmes are relief-oriented rather than poverty eradication programmes. In this context, IRDP acts as a more appropriate anti-poverty programme to fulfil the requirements of enhancing the equality of life of the rural poor in terms of generating additional income and employment opportunities on a permanent basis.

Table 4.6a : Physical Achievements of Rural Development Programmes during 1992-93 and 1993-94 in Karnataka

Programme	Unit	Eighth Plan 1992–97	1992-93		1993-94	
			T	A	T	A
1. IRDP						
a) Benficiary Identified	Lakh No.	5.12	0.86	1.04	1.37	1.37
b) Beneficiary Assistants	,,	5.12	0.86	1.04	1.37	1.33
c) SC/ST Beneficiaries	,,	2.66	0.56	0.40	0.69	0.50
d) TRYSEM	,,	0.70	0.14	0.13	0.10	0.15
2. DWCRA (No. of groups organised)		1132	480	580	650	590
3. JRY Employment generated	Lakh Mandays	2511	441	418	781	588
4. Employment Assurance Scheme : DPAP	,,	NA	NA	NA	132	32
5. Assistance to Surplus Land grantees	No.	13698	2240	2770	2720	2486
6. 100 wells programmes	No.	23680	5097	6163	4833	5961
7. Integrated Rural Energy Programme	No.	178600	NA	NA	42137	26078
8. Rehabilitation of Bonded	No.	800	NA	NA	192	774

Note : T = Target A = Achievements

Source : Related issues of Draft Annual Plans, Government of Karnataka, Bangalore Labourers

PROGRESS OF IRDP IN KARNATAKA

IRDP is the single largest anti-poverty programme being implemented. Initially, it was implemented in a few blocks of the country in 1978-79. It was extended to all the blocks by 2nd October, 1980. In Karnataka, as per the annual reports of the Department of Rural Development, the actual implementation of IRD programme began in 1980-81 covering all the blocks in the State. The physical and financial targets and achievements of IRDP during the Sixth and Seventh Plans may be seen from Table 4.7.

The financial achievements to the target show a declining trend during the Seventh Plan. Over a period of 10 years (from 1980-81 to 1989-90) about 1.51 million beneficiaries (both old and new) have been covered under IRDP and a total amount of Rs. 607.33 crores has been spend (loan + subsidy) in Karnataka. The cumulative percentage of SC/ST beneficiaries covered was 26 per cent of the total, which is less than the prescribed Government norm of 30 per cent (Department of Rural Development : 1987). However, the coverage of SC/ST beneficiaries to total has increased in the successive years. Similarly, the coverage of women beneficiaries, and schemes under Industries, Service and Business (ISB) sector also increased significantly. The credit disbursed per beneficiary also has increased over a period of time (Table 4.7).

Table 4.7 : Progress under IRDP in Karnataka

Year	Achievement of Target (percentage)		Percentage to total Beneficiaries			Per Capita Investment made (Rs.)
	Physical	Financial	SC/ST	ISB	Women	
1980-81	104	105	16	---	---	2943
1981-82	83	109	19	---	---	3983
1982-83	170	123	28	---	---	3271
1983-84	193	138	28	---	---	2861
1984-85	174	155	27	27	8	3508
1985-86	142	118	25	30	13	3876
1986-87	100	112	26	32	17	4554
1987-88	99	104	26	39	23	3301
1988-89	113	101	28	NA	25	5483
1989-90	105	87	29	42	29	5812
1990-91	114	89	NA	NA	NA	5754

Source : Compiled from Annual Reports of Rural Development Department, Government of Karnataka, Bangalore.

Table 4.8 furnishes the details of physical achievements of the targets fixed since 1980-81 to 1990-91. It is clear from the Table that physical achievement has exceeded the targets set in almost all the years. The achievement of number of beneficiaries assisted to

Table 4.8 : Physical Achievement of Target Under IRDP in Karnataka

Year	No. of Beneficiaries		% of Achieve-ment to Target
	Target	Achievement	
1980-81	105000	108893	104
1981-82	105000	87460	83
1982-83	105000	178856	170
1983-84	105000	202228	193
1984-85	105000	182651	174
1985-86	105000	148794	142
1986-87	145500	145275	99
1987-88	161239	159135	99
1988-89	137794	156176	113
1989-90	134088	140275	105
1990-91	109482	125027	114

Source : Same as Table 4.7.

the target during the Sixth Plan (1980-85) was higher (145 per cent) as compared to the Seventh Plan (110 per cent) achievement. Giving second or supplementary assistance to the old beneficiaries started in 1985-86.

The purpose of sanctioning more than one assistance is to enable those who could not cross the poverty line either because of inadequacy of assistance or untimely loss of assets.

Table 4.9 indicates the financial progress of IRDP in terms of total allocation and actual expenditure made under IRDP. The financial allocation made has increased over the years in the State. The percentage of expenditure to the allocation during the Sixth and Seventh Plans was 129 per cent and 102 per cent, respectively.

The performance of IRDP both in terms of physical and financial achievements was higher than the target in all the districts in general and the Southern districts in particular. A similar trend also emerges in the case of percentage of expenditure to allocation under IRDP.

The credit disbursed per beneficiary from 1980-81 to 1990-91 across the districts and also for the State as a whole shows

Table 4.9 : Financial Progress Under IRDP

(Rs. in lakhs)

Year	Allocation	Expenditure	% of Achievement
1980-81	875.000	917.460	105
1981-82	1050.00	1144.198	109
1982-83	1400.000	1722.630	123
1983-84	1400.000	1934.310	138
1984-85	1400.000	2166.003	155
1985-86	1726.560	2043.067	118
1986-87	2173.820	2324.795	112
1987-88	2593.468	2709.386	104
1988-89	2973.300	2990.546	101
1989-90	3444.336	2987.307	87
1990-91	3444.336	3076.529	89

Source : Same as Table 4.7.

fluctuations. It may be noted that in the beginning of the Sixth and Seventh Plans a higher per capita investment was made in almost all the districts.

The percentage of SC/ST beneficiaries covered was 26 per cent to the total, which is less than the prescribed Government norm of 30 per cent (Department of Rural Development, 1987). However, the coverage of SC/ST beneficiaries to the total has increased over the years. Uttara Kannada district shows relatively low coverage while Bangalore, Chitradurga and Gulbarga districts record a consistent increase in assisting SC/STs beneficiaries, much above the norm. The coverage of women beneficiaries and ISB beneficiaries has been given importance since 1984-85 in Karnataka. The norm prescribes that 30 per cent of the beneficiaries should be women. The number of women beneficiaries assisted to the total beneficiaries increased in recent years across the districts and even at the State level also.

Similarly, schemes under ISB sector also show an increasing trend since 1984-85. The beneficiaries assisted under ISB sector to the total beneficiaries clearly show an increasing trend in all the districts and also at the State level. The trend that emerges from this is that non-farm activities are beginning to get good encouragement in rural Karnataka under IRDP.

II

PROFILE OF THE STUDY AREA AND BENEFICIARIES

In the following paragraphs the profile of the selected blocks, villages and IRDP beneficiaries of the study is outlined.

Data for this section is taken from the secondary sources (Census Hand Books, Village Records etc.) and from primary data collected from selected villages and beneficiares.

The blocks are delineated as developed and backward blocks as mentioned in Chapter 3. The details of the selected indicators in these blocks are given in Table 4.10.

DEVELOPED BLOCKS

Table 4.10 indicates that the total geographical area of the developed blocks ranges between 0.44 lakh hectares to 1.64 lakh hectares (Census Hand Books : 1981). The details of Sakleshpur block are not available because it was earlier a part of Manjrabad taluk in Chikamangalur district. It was separated and was formed as a block in 1986. The number of villages in a block varies between 49 (in Sringeri block) and 365 (in Hosakote block).

The total population in a block ranged between .32 lakhs and 2.46 lakhs in these blocks. Further, the percentage of the rural population is about 66 per cent to total population. The percentage of SC/STs to total population ranges from 14 to 25 in developed blocks and 9 to 47 in backward blocks in the study area. The literacy rate (rural vaired) between 53 per cent in Sringeri block and 20 per cent in Bidar.

The percentage of cultivable area to total area was the lowest (12 per cent) in Sringeri block which is covered by vast forest and the highest in Hosakote block (84 per cent). Though Virajpet and Somwarpet blocks in Coorg district also have plantation zone characteristics, the percentage of cultivable area was more than in Sringeri block.

Regarding amenities like education, more than 74 per cent of the villages have schools, but only less than 6 per cent of the villages have schools, but only less than 6 per cent of the villages have

Table 4.10 : Selected Indicators of the Blocks in the Study Area

S. No.	Blocks	Total pop. 1981 (in lakhs)	% of rural pop. to total pop.	% of rural lite-racy rate	% of SC/ST to total popu-lation	% of culti-vable area to total area	% of irri-gated area to total culti-vable area	Number (%) of villages having one or more of the following amenities					
								Educa-tion	Medical	P & T	Comm-unication	App-roach by pucca road	Power supply
DEVELOPED													
1.	Somwarpet	1.64	84	44	17	75	1.37	79	5	45	56	72	70
2.	Virajpet	1.80	88	46	24	50	.30	94	15	75	59	78	63
3.	Saklespur	NA	NA	NA	NA	NA	NA	NA	NA	NA	NA	NA	NA
4.	Sringeri	.32	86	53	14	12	12.57	83	6	19	28	51	64
5.	Hosakote	2.04	79	35	25	84	14.86	74	5	12	57	56	100
6.	Bidar	2.48	68	20	NA	75	8.10	91	6	43	38	38	99
BACKWARD													
1.	Gulbarga	4.03	45	35	22	92	1.06	98	6	47	44	26	74
2.	Sedam	1.29	88	30	27	24	2.16	96	8	36	27	36	71
3.	C. R. Patna	2.18	90	32	10	66	8.84	79	6	17	28	57	86
4.	Haveri	1.82	80	33	15	89	3.16	100	24	38	44	52	91
5.	Hangal	1.70	90	39	18	91	24.33	94	8	30	38	51	94
6.	Hukkeri	2.72	85	31	18	73	9.62	99	4	50	66	72	98

Contd..

Table 4.10 : Contd.

S. No.	Blocks	Total pop. 1981 (in lakhs)	% of rural pop. to total pop.	% of rural literacy rate	% of SC/ST to total population	% of cultivable area to total area	% of irrigated area to total cultivable area	Number (%) of villages having one or more of the following amenities					
								Education	Medical	P & T	Communication	Approach by pucca road	Power supply
BACKWARD													
7.	Khanpur	1.85	90	34	9	42	8.44	96	7	20	21	25	43
8.	B. Bagewadi	2.20	91	32	19	94	4.02	95	4	53	52	61	73
9.	Bilgi	.98	90	26	31	77	11.00	92	13	53	64	83	97
10.	Mudigere	1.13	88	38	26	72		73	8	24	58	55	89
11.	Jaglur	1.11	91	32	42	69	7.53	98	6	28	50	72	83
12.	Challakere	2.19	89	27	47	73	11.72	87	11	34	87	58	99
13.	Nelamangala	1.65	92	36	24	84	10.07	82	5	14	31	52	87
14.	Basavakalyan	2.00	83	22	NA	90	4.63	98	7	55	45	37	36

Note : a. Figures are rounded up to the nearest number.

b. Sakleshpur block separated from a part of Manjarbad block in Chikamangalor district. Hence Sakleshpur block figures are not available.

Source : Census of India 1981, District Census Hand Books, Series 9 Karnataka, Parts. XIII A & B, Village and Town Directory.

medical facilities in developed blocks. The availability of communication and post and telegraph services also varies across blocks. Except in Bidar block, more than 50 per cent of the villages in the rest of the blocks have got pucca roads. Villages of Hosakote and Bidar blocks are fully electrified, while the proportion is less than 70 per cent in other blocks.

BACKWARD BLOCKS

The blocks vary in size of population, area and the number of villages. More than 80 per cent of the people in these blocks, except in Gulbarga, live in rural areas (Table 4.10).

The percentage of literacy rate (rural) was lower, (less than 40 per cent) in the backward blocks as compared to the developed blocks.

The percentage of cultivable area to total area was more in backward blocks than in developed blocks. Among the backward blocks, the percentage of irrigated area to total cultivable area was more in Hangal (24.73 per cent) and the lowest in Gulbarga block (1.06 per cent).

Regarding amenities like education, medical, post and telegraph, and power supply there is not much difference between the two types of blocks. In communications and type of road, the developed blocks are better placed than the backward blocks.

Since the block level data do not capture the village level diversities in the characteristics of the study area, it was decided to present the characteristics of villages coming under different agro-climatic zones. The sample households fall under these villages.

VILLAGE CHARACTERISTICS

The selected 40 villages are broadly grouped under 4 different agro-climatic zones. The zone-wise village characteristics are given in the following paragraphs.

VILLAGES UNDER NORTH DRY ZONE (NDZ)

The blocks included under NDZ are Gulbarga, Sedam, Haveri, Hukkeri, Biligi, and Basavana Bagewadi. The type of soils in the above blocks vary from medium black to deep black, alkaline and sand mixed red soils. The rainfall is generally (less than normal annual average rainfall of 1139 mm.) very low and also irregular

(Directorate of Economics and Statistics: 1991). Generally, the above blocks are droughtprone and quite often face scarcity of cereals and fodder. During summer season the mercury reaches more than 45°C.

The principal crops grown in NDZ under irrigated condition are jowar, hybrid cotton, mexican wheat, and hybrid maize. Under dry cultivation jowar, tur, cotton, groundnut, and chillies are predominantly grown. The staple food in these blocks is jowar. The NDZ's prosperity is limited because of drought-prone conditions causing low crop yields.

The village settlements in NDZ are distinctly different from other zones. Normally, the distance between one village and another village is about 20 to 25 kilometers. Table 4.11 provides details about the characteristics of villages selected in NDZ. By and large, the average population of the selected villages varies between 525 and 5,540, according to 1981 census.

With regard to literacy rates, the village Nandur B Tanda in Gulbarga district which is dominated by Scheduled Caste families has the lowest literacy rate i.e., 16 per cent.

The cultivators percentage to main workers varies between 14 and 55 per cent. The higher percentage of cultivators in Bellambi in Shellabur is due to the higher proportion of irrigated area to total cultivated area.

As far as the amenities are concerned, for example, none of the villages in NDZ has a veterinary hospital. For Veterinary services villagers have to travel a distance ranging from 1 km. to 14 km. Four villages have milk co-operative socieities and the people in the rest of the villages have to travel 2 kms. to 5 kms. to avail themselves of the benefits of milk societies.

All the villages in the zone were within the jurisdiction of branches of the nationalised banks and grameen banks. But, except Ingleshwar (Basawana Bagewadi block of Bijapur district), for all other villages the bank branches were located at a distance of more than 5 kms.

For availing of marketing facilities, the villagers had to travel more than 5 km. Out of 11, 6 villages had bus facilities while people in other villages walked 5 kms. to reach a bus stop. The urban influence on villages in NDZ also seems to be weak because the

Table 4.11 : Some Characteristic Features of the Selected Villages in North Dry Zone

S. No.	Villages	Total Population	Literacy rate %	Cultivators as % main workers	Irrigated area as % total cultivated area	Distance of vet. hospital (km.)	Distance of milk society (km.)	Distance of bank (km.)	Distance of market (km.)	Bus-stand/ Railway Station (km.)	Distance of nearby town (km.)	Type of road
1.	Ingleshwar	5540	33	47	1	10	5	0	0	BS	12	PR
2.	Mannikere	1334	26	45	2	6	5	10	–(5–10)	–(–5)	8	KR
3.	Dharampur	916	36	37	1	1	0	10	10+	BS	16	KR
4.	Chikkalingadahalli	1781	24	34	1	3	3	5	–(–5)	BS	5	PR
5.	Hombardi	1661	41	48	6	3	0	10	–(5–10)	–(–5)	8	KR
6.	Bellambi	3238	24	53	23	4	3	6	–(–5)	BS	10	PR
7.	Masbinal	3952	32	51	2	10	5	11	–(5–10)	BS	10	PR
8.	Shellapur	753	26	50	23	5	0	5	–(–5)	–(–5)	8	KR
9.	Yadahalli	525	24	14	—	10	3	8	–(–5)	–(–5)	7	KR
10.	Habal T	1810	17	35	—	14	0	8	–(–5)	–(–5)	11	KR
11.	Nandur B Tanda	1034	16	55	—	3	2	10	10+	BS, RS	11	PR
12.	Girisagar	3258	30	51	–	12	5	10	0	BS	11	PR

Note : a) BS = Bus Stand, RS = Railway Station, PR = Pucca Road and KR = Kachha Road.

b) Amenities available (if not available within the village, a dash (–) indicates in the column and next to it in brackets, the distance in broad ranges viz., 5 kms. 5–10 kms. and 10 + kms. of the nearest place where the facility is available is given.

c) Main workers includes cultivators, agircultural labourers, household industries, manufacturing, processing, services and repairs and other workers (as defined in the Census Book).

Source : Compiled from concerned District Census Hand Books of 1981 and from Village Records/Schedule.

selected villages are situated at a distance of 5 to 16 kms. from the nearest town.

VILLAGES UNDER SOUTH DRY ZONE (SDZ)

The development blocks that fall in the SDZ are Hosakote, Nelamangala, Chellakere, Jagalur, and Channarayapatna, Generally, the soils vary from sand mixed red laterites to sand mixed black soil. Except Channarayapatna where the Hemavati river flows, the rest of the blocks are dry with low rain fall. The main crops grown in this zone are ragi, paddy, groundnut, coconut, jowar and sugarcane.

The proportion of irrigated are to total cropped area in Bediganahalli was 26 per cent (Channarayanapatna taluk) followed by Kalenahalli (14 per cent), Sonnallipura (12 per cent) and Ghataparthi (12 per cent) (Table 4.12). Whereas in all other villages it is less than 10 per cent, in a few villages the irrigated area is almost nil. Interestingly, there was no cultivable waste in Thippasettyhalli in Nelamangala block of Bangalore district. This village has better transport facilities, the population belongs to one community called Thigala who are most enterprising and grow commercial crops and vegetables.

The caste composition in these villages shows that vokkaligas, lingayats and thiglas, kurubas and SC/STs are the important castes found in the SDZ villages. As compared to the NDZ villages, the villages in the SDZ are relatively small, with less than 1,000 population in 1981, with the exception of 3 villages.

The literacy rate varies between 15 and 54 per cent in these villages. Also a higher percentage of literacy may be seen in villages with a smaller population.

As far as amenities like veterinary hospital are concerned, 50 per cent of the villages in the SDZ do have the above services in the village itself and the rest are located within 5 kms. radius. The milk cooperative societies were found in 5 out of 10 villages and the rest had them within a radius of less than 5 kms.

Commercial banks and Grameen Banks are functioning in 3 villages viz., Pallagatta in Jagalur block, Chitranayakanahalli in Chellekere block and Thippasettyhalli in Nelamangala block. The rest of the villages were less than 5 kms. away from the locations of credit institutions.

Table 4.12 : Some Characteristic Features of the Selected Villages in the Study Area in South Dry Zone

S. No.	Villages	Total Population	Literacy rate %	Cultivators as % main workers	Irrigated area as % total cultivated area	Distance of vet. hospital (km.)	Distance of milk society (km.)	Distance of bank (km.)	Distance of market (km.)	Bus-stand/ Railway Station (km.)	Distance of nearby town (km.)	Type of road
1.	Pallagatta	2680	32	44	1	0	0	0	0	BS	22	PR
2.	Chitranayakanahalli	1794	21	44	4	0	4	0	10+	BS	21	PR
3.	Sonnallipura	804	54	82	12	0	0	4	–(–5)	BS	10	PR
4.	Bediganahalli	642	18	52	28	8	0	5	–(5–10)	–(–5)	8	PR
5.	Kalenahalli	203	5	100	14	6	5	5	–(–5)	BS	4	PR
6.	Ghataparthi	3815	24	50	12	4	4	4	10+	BS	29	PR
7.	Thippasettyhalli	367	21	97	9	0	0	0	–(–5)	–(–5)	19	PR
8.	Karehalli	545	33	67	5	4	4	4	–(–5)	–(–5)	20	PR
9.	Kamblipura	857	34	73	7	0	0	44	–(5–10)	BS	11	KR
10.	Urlakatta	684	36	52	1	4	4	4	–(–5)	–(–5)	28	KR

Note : Same as Table 4.11.

Source : Compiled from concerned District Census Hand Books of 1981 and from Village Records/Schedule.

The distance to markets varied in these villages. Except in one village where market facility exists, the other villages are located at a distance of less than 5 kms.

Regarding transport facilities like bus services, while six villages have this, the people of other villages have to walk upto 5 kms. to reach the bus stop. Except in two villages where only kachha roads are there, in other villages pucca road exists. By and large the villages are located at a distance of more than 10 kms. from the nearest towns.

VILLAGES IN TRANSITION ZONE (TZ)

In the TZ, there are 8 villages which come under four blocks, namely, Bidar, Basavakalyan, Khanapur, and Hangal. The main type of soils are black, black cotton alkaline and sand mixed red soils. Normally, the rain fall is better than in the NDZ. The cropping pattern in the TZ is similar to that of the NDZ.

Out of eight, five villages do not have any irrigation and in the remaining three villages irrigated area ranges from 19 per cent to 49 per cent of the total cultivated area (Table 4.13). The pattern that appears is that the higher percentage of irrigated area is associated with the higher proportion of cultivators to main workers in the TZ villages.

Though the village settlements and the size of population vary marginally, they resemble villages in the NDZ. According to the 1981 census, the size of population range between 457 and 2,532 in these villages (Table 4.13). The literacy rate varied between 15 to 38 per cent.

The infrastructure facilities like vetrinary hospital are located more than 5 kms. away from the selected villages in the TZ. Similarly, milk cooperative societies were functioning within a radius of 5 kms. (except in Linganmath of Khanapur block). Further, markeing facilities were located at a distance of more than 5 kms. away from these villages. The distance between nearby towns and villages is also relatively high.

The availability of transport facilities (bus services) within 5 kms. has relationship to the type of road (pucca). In other words, kachha road means no bus services.

Table 4.13 : Some Characteristic Features of the Selected Villages in the Study Area in Transition Zone

S. No.	Villages	Total Population	Literacy rate %	Cultivators as % main workers	Irrigated area as % total cultivated area	Distance of vet. hospital (km.)	Distance of milk society (km.)	Distance of bank (km.)	Distance of market (km.)	Bus-stand/ Railway Station (km.)	Distance of nearby town (km.)	Type of road
1.	Linganmath	1791	37	42	22	10	0	0	-(-5)	BS	2	PR
2.	Gundenath	2532	25	62	19	10	2	5	-(-5)	-(-5)	16	PR
3.	Shadeguppi	1513	38	63	49	7	0	7	-(5–10)	-(5–10)	20	KR
4.	Kondaji	1200	29	47	---	5	2	5	10+	BS	23	PR
5.	Chikpeth	457	15	14	---	6	4	4	-(-5)	BS	4	PR
6.	Benakanahalli	989	20	43	1	6	6	6	-(5–10)	BS	9	KR
7.	Kherda'b	2157	17	48	---	10	2	10	-(-5)	BS	44	PR
8.	Kinni	1567	17	65	---	12	12	12	-(-5)	-(-5)	19	KR

Note : Same as Table 4.11.

Source : Compiled from concerned District Census Hand Books of 1981 and from Village Records/Schedules.

VILLAGES IN PLANTATION ZONE (PZ)

Unlike other zones, PZ represents altogether different agro-climatic conditions because of hilly terrain. The blocks which are under the PZ are Sringeri, Sakleshpur Mudigere, Virajpet and Somwarpet. The soil varies from sand mixed alluvial to red and brown soils. The main crops grown in the PZ are paddy, cardamom, pepper, coffee and arecanut.

There are ten villages spread over five blocks in the PZ. Except in two villages viz., Byakravally and Kyamanahally in Sakleshpur blocks, the availability of irrigation is either little or nil. The rainfall is very high (more than 2,000 mm) in the PZ as compared to the other three zones. The non-farm activities like bee-keeping and basket knitting were also found in this zone. In three villages, no cultivable waste land was reported. In other villages, it varied from 2 per cent to 21 per cent (Table 4.14).

The houses are isolated and village settlements are not similar to those in other zones. The type of houses (tiled roof) are different, as compared to the other zones (mudwalls with granite/slab roof).

The veterinary hospitals are located at a distance of 3 to 18 kms. The milk co-operative societies are located at less than 6 kms. distance from these villages. The market places are located 5 kms. away from these villages. And 50 per cent of the villages have bus services and the rest of the villagers have to travel at least 5 kms. to reach the bus stops. By and large, villages having pucca roads have transport services.

The summarised characteristic feature of those villages are given in Table 4.14.

The types of soil and crops grown vary across the agro-climatic zones in the study area. The caste composition discloses clearly that lingayats and vokkaligas (along with other backward caste and scheduled caste) can be found in the northern and southern districts in rural Karnataka. Around 88 per cent of the selected villages do not have veterinary services, but they are located at a distance of more than 5 kms. Marketing of the product generated by the IRDP asset (except milk in the SDZ villages) seems to be very weak because the market places and towns are far away from these villages. The credit institutions (except 20 per cent of the villages) are away (more than 5 kms) from the selected villages.

Table 4.14 : Some Characteristic Features of the Selected Villages in the Study Area in Plantation Zone

S. No.	Villages	Total Population	Literacy rate %	Cultivators as % main workers	Irrigated area as % total cultivated area	Distance of vet. hospital (km.)	Distance of milk society (km.)	Distance of bank (km.)	Distance of market (km.)	Bus-stand/ Railway Station (km.)	Distance of nearby town (km.)	Type of road
1.	Byakravally	814	32	34	21	3	3	5	-(-5)	BS	15	PR
2.	Kyamanahally	693	48	17	11	18	3	5	-(-5)	BS	14	PR
3.	Mudigere	934	49	10	--	3	0	0	-(-5)	-(-5)	0	PR
4.	Lokavalli	337	25	5	--	3	2	0	-(-5)	-(-5)	2	PR
5.	Vykuntapura	745	54	41	5	6	2	4	-(-5)	-(-5)	5	PR
6.	Kochavalli	533	63	64	1	12	6	12	-(5–10)	-(-5)	8	KR
7.	Kottoli	832	45	42	--	6	6	10	-(-5)	-(-5)	5	KR
8.	Kedamallur	2135	60	43	--	6	6	10	-(5–10)	BS	13	PR
9.	Takeri	1560	53	43	--	10	6	10	-(5–10)	-(-5)	10	KR
10.	Kirgandur	1930	31	8	--	10	6	10	-(5–10)	-(-5)	10	PR

Note : Same as Table 4.11.

Source : Compiled from concerned District Census Hand Books of 1981 and from Village Records/Schedules.

Many villages are drought-prone. The marginal farmers and agricultural labourers migrate to nearby places for wage employment during droughts.

SOCIO-ECONOMIC CHARACTERISTICS OF SELECTED IRDP

Beneficiaries

This section deals with the socio-economic and demographic features of the IRDP beneficiaries. The purpose here is to analyse the characteristics of the beneficiary households who hail from different agro-climatic zones and also across the status of blocks.

Table 4.15 gives some demographic characteristics of the IRDP beneficiary heads of households by level of development of blocks. The majority of the beneficiaries (140 out of 200) come under backward blocks. The distribution of schemes by sex shows that women beneficiaries account for less than 10 per cent of the total beneficiaries.

The IRDP beneficiary heads of households by age reveal that more than 60 per cent of them had crossed the age of 40 years.

The size of the family of the beneficiaries reveals that only 6 per cent of these families have two members,while more than 70 per cent of the IRDP beneficiaries have more than 5 members in their family. The rest of the families (24 per cent) are in the size class of three and four. The families with single earning member accounted for 16 per cent of the households,while 67 per cent of the families have two earning members. In the backward blocks, 70 per cent of the households have two earning members. By and large, the main occupation reported by a majority of the IRDP households (Table 4.16) was *coolie* (manual labour).

Families with 3 or more dependent members accounted for 52 per cent of the total households. But the distribution across the blocks shows that such families are more (58 per cent) in the backward blocks than in the developed blocks (37 per cent). The dependents in these families were found to be mainly children rather than old persons.

The asset structure, occupation and literacy levels are shown in Table 4.16. The small and marginal farmers put together account for 48 per cent of the total IRDP households. While 46 per cent of the beneficiary families belong to the landless category,about

Table 4.15 : Demographic Characteristics of IRDP Beneficiaries by Type of Blocks

Indicators	Developed blocks	% to total	Backward blocks	% to total	Combined	% to total
1. Total IRDP beneficiary household	60	30	140	70	200	100
2. Sex : Male	54	90	130	184	92	
Female (Heads of HHs)	6	10	10	7	16	8
3. Age group						
Upto 30	9	15	18	13	27	14
31 – 40	14	23	30	21	44	22
41 – 50	7	12	54	39	61	31
51 +	30	50	38	27	68	34
4. Size of the Family						
Upto 2	3	5	10	7	13	6
3 – 4	15	25	32	23	47	24
5 – 6	25	42	51	36	76	38
7 +	17	28	47	34	64	32
5. No. of Dependents						
0	3	5	18	13	21	11
1	8	13	12	8	20	10
2	17	28	29	21	46	23
3	15	25	28	20	43	22
4+	7	12	53	38	60	30
6. No. of earning members						
1	11	18	22	16	33	16
2	36	60	98	70	134	67
3 & above	13	22	20	14	33	17

Source : Household Schedule.

6 per cent of them have 5 or more than 5 acres of land. Across the blocks, 8 per cent (11) of the households in backward blocks have more-than 5 acres of land. The landless households are more (i.e. 56 per cent) in developed blocks than in the backward blocks (41 per cent).

The distribution of IRDP households by main occupation exhibits that Agricultural Labourer households account for a higher

Table 4.16 : Asset Structure, Literacy and Occupation of IRDP Beneficiaries by Type of Blocks

Indicators	Developed blocks	% to total	Backward blocks	% to total	Combined	% to total
1. Land Holdings						
A. Medium farmers & above	1	2	11	8	12	6
B. Small farmers	9	15	40	29	49	24
C. Marginal farmers	16	27	31	22	47	24
D. Landless	34	56	58	41	92	46
2. Main Occupation						
A. Agricultural Labourer	50	83	61	44	111	56
B. Agriculture	8	13	55	39	63	31
C. Non-Agricultural/ Business	2	3	24	17	26	13
3. Literacy						
i) Adults						
A. Literates	12	20	28	20	40	20
B. Illiterates	48	80	112	80	160	80
ii) Children						
A. School/College attending	22	37	44	31	66	33
B. Not sending for school	38	63	96	69	134	67
4. Cattle Owned						
A. Pair of bullocks	4	7	14	10	18	9
B. Bullock cart	2	3	8	9	15	8
C. Cow No.	5	8	24	17	29	15
D. Buffalo	2	3	26	19	28	14
E. Sheep	60	99	130	100	200	100
F. Goat	60	100	140	100	200	100

Source : Household Schedule.

share (83 per cent) in the developed blocks than in the backward blocks (44 per cent), the overall percentage being 56 per cent. Households pursuing agriculture and non-farm activities account for 39 per cent and 17 per cent in the backward blocks, respectively. The same proportions are less in the developed blocks.

In both the blocks, the literacy rate among adults is around 20 per cent. It can be found that the proportion of households sending children to school/college (33 per cent) was also almost the same across the blocks.

Regarding the cattle population owned by these households, 18 per cent owned one pair of bullocks in their house before IRDP. These families belong to the groups of small and medium farmers.

The households which had the milch animals i.e., cows and buffaloes before IRDP, accounted for 12 per cent each. About 10 per cent and 31 per cent of IRDP beneficiaries had sheep and goats, respectively, before IRDP. The number of goats owned was more in the developed blocks than in the backward blocks.

The socio-economic-demographic characteristics of IRDP beneficiaries reveal the following: In the initial period of IRDP implementation there appears to have been a gender bias (only 10 per cent of the women beneficiaries covered to total beneficiaries). The beneficiaries productive age was not taken into consideration (60 per cent of them had crossed 40 years of age) while sanctioning the schemes. More than 70 per cent of the households had 5 members in the family and 67 per cent had two earning members mostly, engaged as *coolies* (manual labourers). Further, more than 52 per cent of the households had 3 or more dependents in the study area and most of the dependents were in the age group 1 - 14.

About 46 per cent of the IRDP beneficiaries were neither owning nor cultivating the land. Though a few identified beneficiaries (mostly in NDZ) had more than 5 acres of land, around 17 per cent and 2 per cent of the beneficiaries had non-farm activities as their main occupation in backward blocks and developed blocks, respectively. 80 per cent of the beneficiaries belonged to the illiterate category. About 18 per cent of the total beneficiaries had already a pair of bullocks before IRDP and only a few of them owned small ruminants.

Keeping the above background characteristics of the study area and the IRDP beneficiaries selected, the next chapter attempts to assess the socio-economic impact of the programme on the beneficiary households.

5

Socio-Economic Impact of IRDP

Introduction

This chapter attempts to look at the socio-economic conditions of the beneficiaries before and after getting IRDP assistance to examine its impact. This chapter has five sections. In the first section, a brief note on the types of IRDP schemes is given. The regional differences either by the status of the block or the agro-climatic zone as a whole on IRDP are attempted to be explained in sections II and III. The level of participation of women beneficiaries in the programme is discussed in section IV. And in the fifth section the additional income generated by the asset across the social groups, schemes and zones, the income mobility of IRDP households and the resultant Crossing of the Poverty Line (CPL) are examined.

SECTION I

IRDP SCHEMES AND THEIR DISTRIBUTION

The realisation on the part of the successive governments about the rising incidence of poverty in India has resulted in the formulation of alternative strategies and programmes by the Central and State Governments to help the weaker sections, particularly, the Schedule Castes (SCs) and Schedule Tribes (STs). Attempts have been made in successive Plans to reduce the absolute number of people living below the poverty line.

It was understood by the policy makers, development administrators and Social Scientists that the socio-economic condition of the target group in general and SC/STs in particular has not improved as it was expected. Apart from other programmes meant for the weaker sections, IRDP is the most important one which aims at improving the living standards of these groups.

DISTRIBUTION OF IRDP HOUSEHOLDS BY CASTE GROUPS

Table 5.1 shows the distribution of IRDP beneficiaries across the social groups. While SC/STs constituted 35.5 per cent of the total beneficiaries (which is higher than the government norm of 30%), Lingayats and Vokkaligas, the dominant castes, accounted for 19.5 per cent and 11.5 per cent, respectively. The other backward communities accounted for 27 per cent and Muslims constituted about 6.5 per cent of the total beneficiaries.

Table 5.1 : Caste Composition of IRDP Beneficiaries

Caste	No.of IRDP Beneficiaries	Percentage to Total
SC/STs	71	35.5
Lingayats	39	19.5
Vokkaliga	23	11.5
Kuruba	16	8.0
Thigala	5	2.5
Dhobi	5	2.5
Brahmin	2	1.0
Other backward communities	26	13.0
Muslims	13	6.5
Total	**200**	**100.0**

Note : Other backward communities includes Kshathriya (4), Kabbliga (4) Hegde (4) Kuruvala Setty (2) Poojari (2) Kumbar (1) Naleke (1) Golla (1) Vishwa Karma (2) Marathi (1) Rajaput (1) Kambar (1) Ediga (1) Devenga Jadar (1).

Table 5.2 reveals details about IRDP schemes sanctioned to the different caste groups in the study area. The pattern that emerges from Table 5.2 is that, irrespective of the social groups, the beneficiaries have received assitance mainly for dairy scheme (49 per cent) and followed by agricultural schemes like pair of bullocks, bullock cart and pumpset which account for 24 per cent. Agriculture along with dairy accounts for 75 per cent of the total schemes.

It may also be seen that 21 per cent of the beneficaries have availed of the assistance under Industries, Service and Business (ISB) schemes. This shows that irrespective of caste there is poor reception to ISB activities among the beneficiaires. Also, while SC/STs and Kurubas have received assistance for all types of schmes under IRDP, the other economically and socially dominant castes have continued to pursue their traditional occupation i.e. farming and allied activities. It is clear from Table 2 that SC/ST beneficiaries are gradually getting into areas other than their traditional occupations like leather tanning/vending. Out of 71 SC/ST beneficiaries, nearly 65 per cent and 15 per cent have received assistance under dairy and agriculture, respectively.

Table 5.2 : Distribution of IRDP Schemes Among the Social Groups

Social Group	Agri-culture	Dairy	Other Animal hus-bandry	Village Indus-tries	Ser-vices	Trad-ing	Total
SC/STs	11	46	5	4	2	3	71
Lingayats	12	19	-	2	-	6	39
Vokkaliga	11	8	-	-	-	4	23
Kuruba	4	2	3	4	1	2	16
Thigala	1	1	-	-	-	3	5
Dhobi	-	2	-	1	2	-	5
Brahmin	-	2	-	-	-	-	2
Other backward communities	5	12	4	-	-	5	26
Muslims	3	5	1	-	-	4	13
Total	**47**	**97**	**13**	**11**	**5**	**27**	**200**

Table 5.3 indicates the number of IRDP beneficiaries who Crossed the Poverty Line (CPL) by caste/religion. Among the caste groups, more Vokkaligas (78 per cent) have moved above the PL of Rs.3,500. This could be attributed mainly to the type of schemes (land-linked schemes) availed of by them. Over all, 48 per cent of the total beneficiaries (old) have crossed the PL. However, in the case of SC/STs, it is only 34 per cent. This could be attributed to the economic base of the SC/STs households which is poor, as majority of them are agricultural labourers.

Table 5.3: Number of Beneficiaries Crossed Poverty Line

Social Group	Total No.of Benefi-ciaries	No.of Bene-ficiaries CPL	% Crossing PL 3,500
SC/STs	71	24	34
Lingayats	39	19	49
Vokkaliga	23	18	78
Kuruba	16	9	56
Thigala	5	2	40
Dhobi	5	2	40
Brahmin	2	1	50
Other backward communities	26	13	50
Muslims	13	8	62
Total	**200**	**96**	**48**

A cross section analysis between the caste groups and schemes to understand the IRDP impact is attempted in Table 5.4. This Table reveals that dairy and schemes under agriculture accounted for 69 per cent (66 out of 96) of the sample beneficiaries who moved above the PL in the study area. It is interesting to note here that, despite their poor socio-economic background more than 34 per cent (24 out of 71) of the SC/ST beneficiareis have CPL. By and large, a similar trend can be seen among other social groups.

Table 5.4 : Number of Beneficiaries Crossed Poverty Line (Rs.3500) Across the Social Group and Schemes

Social Group	Agri-culture	Dairy	Other Animal hus-bandry	Village Indus-tries	Ser-vices	Trad-ing	Total
SC/STs	6	14	3	--	--	1	24
Lingayats	5	7	--	--	--	7	19
Vokkaliga	8	7	--	--	--	3	18
Kuruba	4	--	2	1	--	2	9
Thigala	1	--	--	--	--	1	2
Dhobi	--	--	--	1	1	--	2
Brahmin	--	1	--	--	--	--	1
Other backward communities	3	4	3	--	--	3	13
Muslims	3	3	1	--	--	1	8
Total	30	36	9	2	1	18	96

SECTION II

IRDP AND DEVELOPMENT BLOCKS

In this section we shall examine the relationship between the level of development of the block and the impact of IRDP schemes in the study area. The blocks are classified based on development score assigned by the study conducted to find out the level of development of blocks in Karnataka (Hemlata Rao: 1984). As per the development score, there are six developed blocks and fourteen backward blocks in the study area (for details see chapter 4).

The distribution of IRDP schemes across the blocks is indicated in Table 5.5. The bulk of the schemes, 89 per cent in developed blocks and 64 per cent in backward blocks, are land-linked. Across the development blocks, milch animals were sanctioned more in number. Though agricultural and allied schemes are the major schemes in both types of blocks, ISB schemes constitute a significant share (35 per cent) in backward blocks when compared to developed blocks.

Table 5.5 : Distribution of IRDP Schemes by Blocks

Scheme	No.of Beneficiaries					
	Deve-loped	% to total	Back-war	% to total	Com-bined	% to total
Agriculture	20	17	44	16	64	16
Dairy	66	55	106	39	172	44
Other Animal Husbandry	20	17	25	9	45	12
Village Industries	1	1	26	10	27	7
Service	3	2	12	4	15	4
Trading	10	8	57	21	67	17
Total **Row %**	**120** **(31)**	**100**	**270** **(69)**	**100**	**390** **(100)**	**100**

Note : **Developed blocks** include Hosakote, Bidar, Sringeri, Virajpet, Somawarpet and Sakalespur.

Backward blocks include Gulbarga, Haveri, Hanagal, Hukkeri, Mudigere, Nelamangala, Jagalur, Chalakere, Khanapur, Basava Kalyan, Sedam, Channaraya Patna, Basavana Bagewadi and Bilgi.

The sustenance of IRDP depends on the acceptance of the scheme by the beneficiaries. Acceptance of the IRDP schemes across the economic category (Rao and Erappa : 1987) is presented in Table 5.6. Out of 200 'old' beneficiaries, 143 (72 per cent) were continuing with the programme in the study area at the time of field work. But across different economic categories, the bottom group has the lowest proportion (64 per cent) of beneficiaries continuing with the IRDP scheme as compared to the middle (75 per cent) and upper (100 per cent) groups. But in terms of repayment of loans made by the beneficiaries, the bottom group show a relatively better performance than their counterparts in other categories across the development blocks (Table 5.6). In the developed blocks in the case of households in the bottom group both the income generated by the asset and its percentage to the initial income are higher (46 per cent) than that of the upper group (table 5.7). In the case of backward blocks, though the average annual income generated by the asset decreases with the status of the economic category, the proportion of income generated to the original income is the highest (71 per cent) for the lowest economic category (Table 5.7).

Table 5.6 : Acceptance of IRDP Schemes by Blocks and Economic Category

Economic Category & Blocks	Total No.of Old Beneficiaries	Continuing	Continuing with some repayment	Continuing and have no overdues
Bottom				
Developed	31	17	16	8
Backward	58	40	37	15
Sub-Total	**89**	**57**	**53**	**23**
Middle				
Developed	26	23	20	7
Backward	75	53	48	16
Sub-Total	**101**	**76**	**68**	**23**
Upper				
Developed	3	3	2	1
Backward	7	7	7	2
Sub-Total	10	10	9	3
Grand Total	200	143	130	49

Table 5.7 : Average Annual Income of the Beneficiaries, Income Generated by the Asset Across the Block and Economic Category

(Post IRDP)

Block	Economic Category	Average annual income of beneficaires	Average income generated by the asset	% income generated by scheme to family income
Developed				
	A	4875	1001	21
	B	2282	1048	46
	C	2303	1056	46
Sub-Total		**2467**	**1149**	**47**
Backward				
	A	3122	1711	55
	B	2719	1459	54
	C	1882	1337	71
Sub-Total		**2067**	**1288**	**62**
Grand Total		**2272**	**1208**	**56**

Note : A = Upper, B = Middle, and C = Bottom.

Finally, the proportion of IRDP beneficiaries crossing the PL across different economic categories and by development status of the block is indicated in Table 5.8. Crossing the PL was arrived at by considering the income from other sources as well as from the IRDP asset. Though it is clear from Table 5.7 that assets availed of by the bottom group generated much higher income than the other two groups in the developed blocks, their number in crossing the PL was less (37 per cent) as compared to the upper and middle groups (Table 5.8). The main reason was that income earned by the bottom groups from all other sources was much less than that of the other groups. In other words, because of the other sources of income being higher in the case of the upper and middle groups, a considerable percentage of them are pushed above the PL. The bottom group beneficiaries in the backward blocks moving above the PL were higher than in the developed blocks. It is also true that the annual income of the IRDP beneficiaries in developed blocks across the schemes was higher than in the backward blocks. This, in fact, has helped a larger more number of IRDP beneficiaries to CPL in the developed blocks.

Table 5.8 : Percentage of IRDP Beneficiaries (old) Crossed the Poverty Line by Blocks and Economic Category

Block	Economic Category	A	B	C	Total
	Poverty Level	CPL %	CPL %	CPL %	CPL %
Developed		100	78	31	54
Backward		67	48	40	45
Total		**71**	**55**	**37**	**48**

Note : A : Upper B: Middle C : Bottom
CPL : Crossing Poverty Line (Rs.3,500).

SECTION III

ZONE-WISE PERFORMANCE OF IRDP IN KARNATAKA

An attempt is made to analyse the data collected for Concurrent Evaluation of IRDP by zones. The purpose is to find out whether different agro-climatic conditions have any influence on the performance of IRDP in rural Karnataka. In other words, it is interesting to study whether the implementing authorities considered the suitability of schemes for different agro-climatic zones. Karnataka State is divided into 10 agro-climatic zones* (Karnataka Gazetteer Part I : 1982, p.593-5). The blocks in the study area come under four zones viz., Northern Dry Zone (NDZ), Southern Dry Zone (SDZ), Transition Zone (TZ) and Plantation Zone (PZ).

The distribution of schemes under IRD programme zone-wise is presented in Table 5.9. Dairy schemes seem to be dominant in all the zones as compared to the other schemes. Among the zones,

Table 5.9 : Distribution of IRDP Beneficiaries by Agro-Climatic Zone and Schemes

Zones/ Schemes	Dairy	Trading	Agriculture	Traditional village industries	Animal Husbandry	Service	Total
NDZ	43 (36)	15 (12)	24 (20)	14 (12)	17 (14)	7 (6)	120 (100)
SDZ	41 (41)	20 (20)	9 (9)	11 (11)	14 (14)	5 (5)	100 (100)
TZ	44 (60)	12 (17)	12 (17)	1 (2)	1 (2)	--	70 (100)
PZ	44 (44)	20 (20)	19 (19)	1 (1)	13 (13)	3 (3)	100 (100)
Total	**172** **(44)**	**67** **(17)**	**64** **(16)**	**27** **(7)**	**45** **(12)**	**15** **(4)**	**390** **(100)**

Note : Figures in bracket denote row percentage to total.

* The Agriculrural Zones in Karnataka
1. The North Eastern Transition Zone
2. The North Eastern Dry Zone
3. The Northern Dry Zone
4. The Northern Transition Zone
5. The Central Dry Zone
6. The Southern Dry Zone
7. The Southern Transition Zone
8. The Eastern Dry Zone
9. The Hilly Zone
10. The Coastal Zone.

in the TZ milch animals account for the major share of the total schemes. Irrespective of zonal peculiarities schemes have been sanctioned. In other words, the agro-climatic condition of a region has not made any influence in the sanctioning of the IRDP schemes to the beneficiaries in the State. Some of the villages had active milk co-operative societies at the time of implementing the IRDP, where-as, in a few other villages,milk co-operatives societies were established as an aftermath of IRDP. This trend was observed during our field visits. Establishment of milk societies newly may be attributed to the organisation of beneficiaries and to the encouragement of officials concerned in the district.

Following dairy schemes, the major share is accounted for by trading and agriculture. It is interesting to note here that village industries are significantly more in NDZ and SDZ than in other zones. Wool weaving (33 per cent) and pottery (29 per cent) are the important activities under village industries in the study area, while goat and sheep units, and piggery units occupy the first and second place under other animal husbandry schemes. All the piggery units sanctioned fall in the PZ. It can be seen here that the cultural peculiarities and food habits of the people in the PZ have made IRDP beneficiaries to opt for piggery. The number of piglets had been reduced by one in the case of the sample households surveyed and the reason given for this was the village festival organised prior to the survey month. Here it can be seen that,on the one hand, culture and its perpetuation through food habits made a few IRDP beneficiaries to reduce their piglets and on the other hand, the economic conditions of the beneficiaries forced some of them to sell the asset to participate in the social functions like village festival.

Table 5.10 provides the details of acceptance level of the schemes by the beneficiaries in different zones. The over all zonal picture reveals that,72 per cent of the beneficiaries are continuing with the scheme and about 25 per cent of the beneficiaries are successful with the programme,having no overdues. Across the zones, the performance of beneficiaries is relatively better in SDZ with regard to continuing with the scheme and also having some repayment of loan. The intra-zone and inter-zone analysis by economic category of the beneficiaries reveals interesting results (Table 5.13). For instance, the bottom group shows relatively better performance than the other two groups in terms of clearing of the loans in all zones except TZ.

Table 5.10 : Acceptance of Schemes by Beneficiaries and Zones

Zones	Old Beneficiaries	Continuing	Continuing with some repayment	Continuing & have no overdues
NDZ	60	39 (65)	37 (62)	9 (15)
SDZ	50	48 (96)	42 (84)	18 (36)
TZ	40	24 (60)	21 (53)	8 (20)
PZ	50	32 (64)	30 (60)	14 (28)
Total	**200**	**143** **(72)**	**130** **(65)**	**49** **(25)**

Note : Figures in brackets refer to row percentage to total.

After examining the general performance of beneficiaries across the economic category by zones, it is pertinent to see how SC/STs and women beneficiaries have fared with the programme in these zones. The details are given in Table 5.11 and 5.12. Across the zones, the performance of SC/ST beneficiaries seems to be better in SDZ as compared to the other zones. The proportion of SC/ST beneficiaries continuing the scheme with some repayment and with no overdues is higher in SDZ as compared to the other zones.

Table 5.11 : Acceptance of Schemes by SC/ST Beneficiaries and Zones

Zones	Old Beneficiaries	Continuing	Continuing with some repayment	Continuing & have no overdues
NDZ	21	14 (67)	14 (67)	4 (19)
SDZ	14	14 (100)	14 (100)	5 (36)
TZ	18	10 (56)	8 (44)	--
PZ	16	13 (81)	12 (75)	3 (19)
Total	**69**	**51** **(74)**	**48** **(70)**	**12** **(6)**

Note : Figures in brackets refer to row percentage to total.

Table 5.12 : Acceptance of Schemes by Women Beneficiaries and Zones

Zones	Old Beneficiaries	Continuing	Continuing with some repayment	Continuing & have no overdues
NDZ	5	3	3	–
SDZ	3	3	3	1
TZ	1	1	1	1
PZ	7	5	5	3
Total	**16**	**12**	**12**	**5**

Note : Figures in brackets refer to row percentage to total.

Among the women beneficiaries, in all 31 per cent of them have no over dues and 75 per cent of them are continuing with the programme with some repayment.

Zone-wise acceptance of IRDP schemes of 200 beneficiaries by economic category is presented in Table 5.13. A little over 50 per cent of the beneficiaries belong to the middle group. The rest are distributed among the bottom (45 per cent) and upper groups (5 per cent). Coming to the percentage of acceptance of the scheme i.e., continuing with the programme, the proportion is higher for the upper (100 per cent) and middle (75 per cent) economic categories than the bottom group (57 per cent). Further, within each economic category, across the zones, fluctuation can be seen. However, the interesting point is that the response of the bottom group in terms of repayment of loan is better than that of the other groups (Table 5.13).

Table 5.14 points out the details of the income generated by the IRDP asset and by other sources by zones and economic category. In TZ the annual income of the upper strata shows that they were above the poverty line (Rs.3,500). It is noteworthy here that the income generated by the IRDP asset and the percentage increase in income favour the bottom group, as compared to the other groups across the zones.

After calculating the additional income generated by the asset on an average, the proportion of families moving above the PL is examined. Altogether, 48 per cent of the beneficiaries crossed the PL. The same proportion in SDZ and PZ is more than 60 per cent. In NDZ it is 42 per cent and 25 per cent in TZ (Table 5.15). The

Table 5.13 : Zone-wise Acceptance of Schemes by Beneficiaries and Economic Category

Zones/ Economic Category	No. of Old Beneficiaries	Percentage (Row) of Acceptance		
		Continuing	Continuing with some repayment	Continuing & have no overdues
Bottom				
NDZ	27	59	56	30
SDZ	15	100	93	33
TZ	22	59	55	14
PZ	25	52	48	28
Sub-Total	**89**	**57**	**53**	**26**
Middle				
NDZ	29	66	62	
SDZ	32	94	78	38
TZ	18	61	50	28
PZ	22	73	73	27
Sub-Total	**101**	**75**	**67**	**23**
Upper				
NDZ	4	100	100	25
SDZ	3	100	100	33
TZ	--	--	--	--
PZ	3	100	67	33
Sub-Total	**10**	**100**	**90**	**30**

reason for relatively more number of beneficiaries crossing the PL in SDZ and PZ is that the initial income of the beneficiaries was close to the poverty line and also, these families had more number of earning members. Among the 'old' beneficiaries (who have availed of the schemes in 1983-84), 90 per cent of them were below the poverty line at the time of taking the loan. In other words, 10 per cent of the beneficiaries were wrongly identified or the leakage rate is 10 per cent. However, the percentage of leakage was reduced to 5 when 'current' beneficiaries were also included at the time of the Concurrent Evaluation. The percentage of leakage was reduced mainly because of the 'Grama sabha' meeting where the 'current' beneficiaries were identified and also the efficiency of the implementing agency (careful assessment of annual income, following prescribed percentage of SC/STs and women beneficiaries coverage).

Table 5.14 : Average Annual Income, Income Generated by the Asset by Economic Category and Zones (After Two Years)

Zones	Economic Category	Average Annual Income	Average Income generated by the asset	Percentage of income increase due to asset
NDZ	A	3044	1828	60
	B	2139	1257	59
	C	2829	1388	49
	ST	**2562**	**1400**	**55**
SDZ	A	2146	1676	78
	B	1637	2356	144
	C	2241	1757	78
	ST	**2058**	**1897**	**92**
TZ	A	--	--	--
	B	1424	778	55
	C	1850	806	44
	ST	**1606**	**791**	**49**
PZ	A	5429	930	17
	B	2603	994	38
	C	2818	1074	38
	ST	**2871**	**1019**	**35**

Note : A : Upper, B : Middle C: Bottom, ST: Sub-Total

Table 5.15 : IRDP (Old) Beneficiaries and their Levels of Poverty by Zones

Zones	TB	BPL	% to Total	APL	% to Total
NDZ	60	52	87	22	42
SDZ	50	45	90	27	60
TZ	40	40	100	10	25
PZ	50	43	86	27	63
Total	**200**	**180**	**90**	**86**	**48**

TB = Total Beneficiaries; BPL = Below Poverty Line;
APL = Above Poverty Line (Rs.3,500).

SECTION IV

IRDP AND WOMEN BENEFICIARIES

This section intends to probe into the impact of IRDP on women beneficiaries.

While examining the status of women with -in class societies, a number of authors have maintained the transformation in traditional economic organisation cause an increased dichotomization of sex roles and concomitant sexual inequalities. Engles (1972, 1984) for example, insisted that the development of private property created a division of labour which diminished the value of female production from social views to private use of the household. In her pioneering work,Boserup (1970) noted that women were often victims of development. She demonstrated that women had been relegated to jobs in the backward sectors of the economy.

The Committee on the Status of Women in India identified that female labour force participation in India was contingent on both cultural and economic conditions (Government of India : 1974). Further, the Committee also highlighted that even when women were employed in occupations outside the home, they tended to fill the lower ranks, received lower wages and had fewer opportunities for training and promotion than men. Even in the industrialised nations like United Kingdom, women are over represented in the ranks of the poor and gender-based disadvantage increased over time (Robert Wright : 1992).

Lynn Benett (1992) also expressed similar opinion that "women are central to the success to the poverty alleviation efforts in the short and long run and market forces have great potential to influence gender ideology and increase the perceived value of women". Further, she said that women are more vulnerable than men. Women should be treated as ` economic agents' and hence women-specific beneficiaries oriented programmes should be thought of. This is because 30 to 35 per cent of the rural families are headed by women (Government of India : 1988) and these families are depending on the income earned by women only.

An attempt is made to know the coverage of women beneficiaires to the total IRDP beneficiaries, their perception on IRDP and their level of participation. To do this we have considered certain indicators like type of schemes sanctioned, percentage of coverage and acceptance of the scheme by the status of the block in rural Karnataka.

Out of 390 beneficiaries (both current and old) only 58 (15 per cent to total) women beneficiaries were given assistance under IRDP (Table 5.16). That means, the coverage of women beneficiaries is below the government norm (30 per cent to total). The distribution of schemes among the women beneficiaries shows that, 64 per cent and 29 per cent of them have received assistance for milch animals and for trading activities respectively. The fact that emerges from Table 5.17 is that in the developed blocks dairy schemes dominate (87 per cent) and the schemes under trading are highly significant i.e. 61 per cent. Now the question that arises is, are the characteristic features of the backward blocks capable enough to provide support to the trading activities to flourish women beneficiaries so that diversifying the rural economy seems to be faster by absorbing the surplus agricultural labourers (particularly women labourers). On the other hand, dairy activity normally acts as a push factor in the developed blocks. For instance, it is clear from Hosakote block (which is one of the developed blocks) where support to factors like milk co-operative society exists in both the selected villages which ultimately land in Mother Dairy in Bangalore, gave a big push to the dairy scheme.

Table 5.16 : Distribution of Women Beneficiaries Under IRDP by Schemes

Scheme	Total beneficiaries	% to total	Women beneficiaries	% to total	% of women beneficiaries
Agriculture	64	16	3	5	5
Dairy	172	44	37	64	22
Other animal husbandry	45	12	-	-	-
Village Industries	27	7	1	2	4
Services	15	4	-	-	-
Trading	67	17	17	29	25
Total	**390**	**100**	**58**	**100**	**15**

Table 5.17 : Schemes received by Women Beneficiaries under IRDP by Blocks

Scheme/ Blocks	Deve-loped	% to total	Back-ward	% to total	Com-bined	% to total
Dairy	26	87	11	39	37	64
Trading	1	3	12	13	13	22
Pair of bullocks	3	10	--	--	3	5
Bangle business	--	--	2	8	2	3
Wool weaving	--	--	1	3	1	2
Tailoring	--	--	1	3	1	2
Cycle Shop	--	--	1	3	1	2
Total	**13**	**100**	**28**	**100**	**58**	**100**

Table 5.18 furnishes the extent of acceptance of IRDP by women beneficiairies across economic categories. Out of 200 old beneficiaries who availed of IRDP during 1983-84, only 16 (8 per cent) are women. Though the coverage of women beneficiairies is initially low; their acceptance level of IRDP schemes across the economic category, particularly middle and upper group, seems to be higher than the bottom group. However, the bottom group also shows promising results (56 per cent) of participating in the schemes and a few among them clear the loans (Table 5.18). Out

Table 5.18 : Acceptance of IRDP Schemes by Women Beneficiaries

(Old beneficiaries)

Indicators	Economic Category			
	Bottom	Middle	Upper	Total
Total beneficiaries covered	89	101	10	200
Women Beneficiaries	9 (10)	6 (6)	1 (10)	16 (8)
Continuing	5 (56)	6 (100)	1 (100)	12 (75)
Continuing with some repayment	5 (56)	6 (100)	1 (100)	12 (75)
Continuing & have no overdues	2 (22)	3 (50)	-- --	5 (31)

Note : Figures in brackets are percentage to total.

of 16 women beneficiaries 5 were continuing with the scheme without any overdues. Out of these 5 beneficiaries, 3 were in developed blocks and 2 in backward blocks.

SECTION V

Investment Productivity Under IRDP :

In this section an attempt is made to study the productivity of IRDP investments by calculating the Incremental Capital Output Ratio (ICOR).

$$\text{ICOR} = \frac{\text{Capital Investment}}{\text{Annual Net Income from the Asset}}$$

Capital investment : includes the loan amount + subsidy and own money invested

Annual net income is arrived at by computing the net income generated by assets per annum.

The ICOR is calculated for IRDP beneficiaries across schemes, castes, status of the block and zones. The annual average net income from the asset is found out after deduction of paid out costs (either in cash or kind, the latter being valued at market prices of the product) from the annual income of the asset. The assumption here is that if the ICOR is low, then the income generated by the asset per unit of investment is more and vice versa. The ICOR helps to arrive at how much of investment and what period will be required to cross the poverty line.

Table 5.19 gives the details of ICOR by schemes for different types of blocks. The ICOR of all the schemes was 2.92 i.e.,to get one rupee of income annually 2.92 units of initial investment were required. But across the blocks, in backward blocks ICOR was 2.61 as against the developed blocks' ratio of 4.31. In other words, to generate one rupee of income annually in the backward blocks, it needs Rs. 2.61 capital investment initially, while in the developed block it is Rs.4.31. The over all ICOR (2.92) in the study area is closer to the assumed ICOR of 2.7 for the Seventh Plan.*

* Kurian (1987) justifies that "most of the IRDP schemes involve rather labour intensive activities. Even then, as against an economy-wide ICOR of about 5 for the Sixth Plan (4 for the Seventh Plan) and ICOR of 1.5 and 2.73 for IRDP investment without sufficient empirical basis was too optimistic. And a number of evaluation studies conducted during the Sixth Plan have confirmed this".

Table 5.19 : ICOR by Schemes and Blocks

Scheme	ICOR		
	Backward Blocks	Developed Blocks	All Blocks
Agriculture	4.20	6.46	4.46
Dairy	3.34	4.07	3.56
Other Animal Husbandry	3.24	3.33	3.25
Village Industries	1.21	0.00	1.25
Services	0.55	0.00	0.55
Trading	0.87	3.78	1.26
Total	2.61	4.31	2.92

The overall ICOR of 2.6 in backward blocks as compared to 4.3 in developed blocks indicates that the productivity of IRDP schemes was relatively higher in the former than in the latter. Further-more, the average investment made per IRDP beneficiary was Rs.2,595 and Rs.3,006 in developed and backward blocks, respectively during 1983-84. The income generated by all the schemes shows that it was more in the backward blocks (Rs.1,154) and less in the developed blocks (Rs.602). It shows that the higher the level of average investment, the greater is the income generation by the asset.

Across the two types of blocks and within the block, different IRDP schemes bring out some interesting ICOR results. For instance, the productivity schemes under agriculture are lower when compared to the other schemes. This is indicated by the higher ICOR in the case of agricultural and allied schemes, as compared to various non-agricultural schemes. The average income generated was more in the case of the latter (Rs.1,740) than the former (Rs.989).

The agro-climatic zonal behaviour on IRDP schemes in terms of asset income generation is presented in Table 5.20. It can be noticed that dry-zones i.e., SDZ and NDZ are more potential in generating additional income (all the schemes) to IRDP beneficiaries than the TZ and PZ. Also across differentzones,the non-farm activities are more productive than the schemes under agriculture, dairy and other animal husbandry schemes.

Table 5.20 : ICOR by Agro-Climatic Zones and Schemes

Scheme	ICOR				
	NDZ	SDZ	TZ	PZ	All Zones
Agriculture	3.80	2.65	15.33	6.84	4.46
Dairy	3.73	3.86	3.26	3.26	3.56
Other Animal Husbandry	3.93	2.37	2.32	3.33	3.25
Village Industries	1.22	1.20	0.00	0.00	1.25
Services	0.00	0.55	0.00	0.00	0.55
Trading	0.52	0.96	0.00	3.50	1.26
Total	**2.61**	**2.27**	**4.63**	**3.97**	**2.92**

The productivity of IRDP schemes by social groups is analysed by calculating the ICOR for caste groups in Table 5.21. The overall picture shows that in backward blocks the productivity for caste groups in terms of additional income generation by the IRDP assets is better than in the developed blocks and more so in the case of those caste groups falling in the lower rungs of the caste hierarchy. Interestingly, IRDP programmes provide a helping hand in terms of income generation, particularly to SC/STs and other backward castes, more than the other caste groups in the study area.

Table 5.21 : ICOR by Caste and Blocks

Caste	ICOR		
	Developed Blocks	Backward Blocks	All Blocks
SC/ST	8.64	3.02	3.61
Ligayat	1.11	2.55	2.38
Vokkaliga	4.14	3.40	3.88
Kuruba	0.00	2.23	2.60
Thigala	0.00	1.04	1.04
Dhobi	3.25	0.00	3.25
Brahmin	7.50	0.00	7.50
Other Backward Castes	3.28	3.30	3.20
Muslims	2.50	2.86	2.78
Total	**4.31**	**2.61**	**2.92**

Table 5.22 exhibits the details of ICOR by agro-cliamtic zones across caste/religion who availed of the IRDP. The capital output ratio per unit of investment in the case of Muslims was higher than others. It means that the scheme like dairy and schemes under agriculture sanctioned to Muslims are relatively more productive. A little over 30 per cent of the schemes sanctioned fall in the trading activity (Table 5.20). Therefore, the income generated by the asset was more. It is an established fact that non-farm activities fare better than land-linked schemes.

Table 5.22 : ICOR by Agro-Climatic Zones and Castes/Religion

Scheme	ICOR				
	NDZ	SDZ	TZ	PZ	All Zones
SC/ST	2.94	2.95	5.71	5.07	3.61
Lingayat	2.09	1.00	5.37	1.11	2.38
Vokkaliga	0.00	3.03	0.00	5.37	3.88
Kuruba	2.94	1.88	3.33	0.00	2.60
Thigala	0.00	0.87	0.00	0.00	1.04
Dhobi	0.00	0.00	10.00	1.56	3.25
Brahmin	0.00	0.00	0.00	2.50	7.50
Other Backward Castes	3.83	1.89	2.56	5.50	3.29
Muslims	1.32	5.10	3.14	2.09	2.78
Total	**2.61**	**2.27**	**4.63**	**3.97**	**2.92**

However, the trend in ICOR in terms of zone and social groups does not seem to be clear. Nevertheless, the SDZ shows higher output ratio among the social groups in general and Lingayats in particular in generating additional income to the rural poor families. IRDP schemes availed of by SC/STs in dry-zones are more productive, as compared to those in TZ and PZ.

The ICOR for different pre-assistance income groups may be seen from Table 5.23. Though there is no clear pattern across income groups, it may be seen that the productivity is higher for the highest income group (Rs 6400 +) than for the other groups. This may be attributed to the characteristic features of the households

Table 5.23 : ICOR by Income Groups and Blocks

Income Group	ICOR Developed Blocks	Backward Blocks	All Blocks
0 - 2265	5.03	2.82	3.27
2266 - 3500	4.28	2.26	2.50
3501 - 4800	3.61	2.97	3.03
4801 - 6400	1.73	7.10	3.08
6400 +	2.67	1.57	1.98
Total	**4.31**	**2.61**	**2.92**

Note : The annual income of the IRDP beneficiaries considered here as assessed by investigator for income classification.

(may be owning land, more number of wage earners, less dependency ratio and high entrepreneurial capabilities).

Incidentally, the zonal behaviour across the income intervals of IRDP in terms of ICOR reveals that the bottom group needs more per capita investment through IRDP assistance than the successive income groups (Table 5.24). The higher the average annual income of the IRDP beneficiaries, the lower shall be the ICOR. A similar trend also holds good across the zones and within the zones.

Table 5.24 : ICOR by Income Groups and Agro-Climatic Zones

Scheme	ICOR NDZ	SDZ	TZ	PZ	All Zones
0 - 2265	2.98	2.41	4.29	4.85	3.27
2266 - 3500	1.85	2.15	6.43	3.90	2.50
3501 - 4800	2.97	0.00	0.00	3.61	3.03
4801 - 6400	0.00	7.10	0.00	1.73	3.08
6400 +	3.33	0.84	0.00	2.67	1.98
Total	**2.61**	**2.27**	**4.63**	**3.97**	**2.92**

INCOME MOBILITY OF IRDP BENEFICIARIES

Table 5.25 provides the details of the income mobility of IRDP beneficiaries by income groups. The income groups are classified, based on the average annual income of the beneficiaries.

Table 5.25 : Income Mobility of IRDP Beneficiaries by Income Groups in Karnataka

Pre-assistance Income Group	Post-Assistance Income Groups					
	0–2265	2266–3500	3501–4800	4801–6400	6400+	Total
0 - 2265	44	38	23	14	4	123
2266 - 3500	3	17	16	11	8	55
3501 - 4800	0	0	4	5	4	13
4801 - 6400	0	0	1	3	0	4
6400 +	0	0	0	1	4	5
Total	**47**	**55**	**44**	**34**	**20**	**200**

Note : Income mobility matrix is arrived by computing annual income assessed by the investigator (Pre-IRDP) and the total annual income (from all sources (Post-IRDP) of IRDP.

This is because, after two years of IRDP assistance i.e., at the time of Concurrent Evaluation, the income generated by the asset and also from all other sources was assessed for comparative purpose to arrive at income mobility of the rural poor households. Out of 200 'old' beneficiaries, 62 per cent (123) belong to the destitutes category (Rs. 0–2,265) at the time of implementing IRDP. Out of these 123 households,44 households i.e., 38 per cent of them, have remained in the same income group even after assistance. By and large, the income mobility of IRDP beneficiaries seems to be positive (in moving at least to the next income group) in the study area.

CONCLUSION

The distribution of land-linked schemes found more in developed blocks. Non-farm schemes, relatively, are more in backward blocks. In the case of backward blocks, though more allied agricultural schemes are sanctioned, the major constraint is the marketing of the produce. Across the economic category, the bottom group repayment of loans helps recycling of money more than the other groups. This is because of higher income generation by the IRDP asset of bottom group beneficiaries. The percentage of asset income to the total annual income was much higher in the case of bottom group beneficiaries and vice versa in the case of other groups. The number of middle and upper group beneficiaries in CPL was more than the bottom group beneficiaries.

In the initial stage of implementation of IRDP, the implementing agency did not give due coverage for women beneficiaries in Karnataka. The schemes that were sanctioned for women beneficiaries are dominated by dairy and trading activities. The schemes sanctioned for women across the blocks show that while dairy-farming scheme was predominent (87 per cent) in the developed blocks, it was trading, in the backward blocks. The trend, however, seems to be encouraging for schemes like dairy in developed blocks. But in terms of continuing with the assets and with no over dues by women beneficiaries, it does not show any such trend.

The implementing agency of IRDP in Karnataka treated the programme in an *ad hoc* manner. The over all picture shows that non-farm schemes fare better (especially in backward blocks) than land-linked schemes (but vice versa in the case of SC/ST beneficiaries). The bottom group beneficiaries across the economic category show more response in repaying the loans, which helps in recycling of the money in the banks than other groups.

While sanctioning IRDP schemes, zonal peculiarities have not been considered by the implementing agency. This is indicated by the dominance of dairy schemes in all the zones. In some villages milk co-operative societies started as an aftermath of IRDP. The milk societies came into existence in some villages because of the efforts of beneficiaries. The poorest of the poor have evinced keen interest in participating and also have succeeded to some extent in CPL across different zones. The percentage of leakage i.e., the non-poor availing of IRDP is lower in the case of current beneficiaries (5 per cent) than old beneficiaries (10 per cent).

Though about 48 per cent of the poor households could cross the poverty line, it has been possible mainly for those who were close to it before getting the assistance. Also, though the overall ICOR is fairly low, a lot of variations could be found across zones, blocks, caste and income groups.

6

Role of Financial Institutions in Implementation of IRDP

In this chapter an attempt is made to bring out a comparative analysis of the working of Commercial Banks (CBs) and Regional Rural Banks (RRBs) in implementing IRDP in the study area.

Credit is one of the important instruments used for alleviating poverty. A strategy has been devised to advance cheap institutional credit to the rural poor. This is being channelised through credit institutions like (CBs), (RRBs) and Co-operatives. Both Union and State Governments are participating in the credit programmes actively, by providing subsidies to the weaker sections. Attempts have been made in the successive Plans to reduce the absolute number of people living below the poverty line. This intervention necessitated designing of various anti-poverty programmes to cover the target group. However, what is depressing is that, despite all these efforts still 29.23 per cent of the population live below the poverty line (Financial Express : 1990). The earlier programmes have not been properly integrated either spatially or functionally. Hence, there has been a wide range of discussion on the basic concept of Integrated Rural Development Programme (IRDP) which was initiated in 1976. A review of literature pertaining to the theoretical base on IRDP shows that there are four approaches to accomplish IRD viz., 1) The Institutional approach of Gunnar Myrdal, (2) The New Economics' approach, (3) The Neo-Marxian approach and (4) The Gandhian approach (G. Parthasarathy : 1982). The central idea in the institutional approach is that "history and politics, theories and ideologies, economic structures and levels, social stratification, agriculture and industry, population development, health and education and so on must be studied not in isolation but in their mutual relationships" (Myrdal : 1970).

The present chapter intends to examine the role of institutional approach in a restricted sense by taking credit as an instrument to eradicate poverty. Myrdal has envisaged the significance of the inter-relationships between the institutions and the attitudes of society and discarded the conventional theory of Development. The level of performance of the two types of credit institutions (CBs and RRBs) in advancing credit to alleviate rural poverty by strengthening the economic base of the weaker sections of the rural households through IRD programmes is examined in this chapter.

HISTORICAL BACKGROUND

The credit system has its own historical background in India. For example, before nationalisation of banks, non-institutional agencies (i.e., money lenders, land-lords etc.) and co-operatives (to some extent) advanced rural credit. Over 90 per cent of the credit needs of the rural poor were met by non-institutional credit agencies (Hanumappa & Ninan : 1982). Even more disconcerting was the fact that, of the total non-institutional credit, over 60 per cent was met by the land-lords-cum-money lenders who are notorious for charging exorbitant rates of interest. It is ironical that inspite of our development Plans, large segments of the rural poor were still at the mercy of the landlords and money lenders for their credit needs (Hanumappa & Ninan : 1982). The All India Rural Credit Survey Committee (AIRCSC) constituted in 1954 found that advances made to agriculture by the Co-operatives and Governments, and CBs were to the tune of 3 per cent and a little less than 1 per cent, respectively (Ojha : 1986, 150). The all India Rural Credit Review Committee (AIRCRC) was appointed in July 1966 to assess the progress made by co-operatives and CBs in advancing credit since 1951-52. The AIRCSC also revealed the high degree (88 per cent) of rural dependence on high cost non-institutional credit. The AIRCRC recommended the establishment of a specialised agency called Small Farmers Development Agency (SFDA) to provide credit to the rural poor (RBI : 1969). The All-India Debt and Investment Survey in 1971 revealed some improvement in institutional credit from 1951-71 for cultivator households, but the position of non-cultivators worsened despite the spread of banking infrastructure (RBI : 1977). As the existing co-operatives were not in a position to meet the demands of the rural people, RBI, as per the policy of the Government of India, decided to involve CBs to advance credit for agriculture, small scale industries, etc., and this was done through the policy of 'Social Control' introduced in 1967. Further, this activity got intensified when 14 major CBs were nationalised on 19th July 1969. The Lead Bank Scheme was also introduced by RBI in 1969 to take care of banking development in various districts. Further, these banks were asked to identify the Growth Centres in each district. Subsequently, 'District Credit Plan' was prepared by each Lead Bank in 1976 for implementation. Nevertheless, all these measures could not help percolation of adequate credit to the rural poor.

In the light of the above experience, the Government of India appointed a study group under the Chairmanship of M. Narasimham to review the credit inflow to the weaker sections. Based on the recommendations of the above study group, the Government of India decided to establish a new chain of credit institutions called Regional Rural Banks in 1975. The need for establishment of RRBs was prompted by the failure of co-operatives and urban-oriented CBs. The prime objective of a RRB is to advance credit to agriculture, small-scale industries etc., on a priority basis to the weaker sections. The Committee to Review Arrangements for Institutional Credit for Agriculture and Rural Development (CRAFICARD) of RBI drew the attention of assisting credit-worthy programmes to the rural poor. According to CRAFICARD (1981) "the normal criterion of banking that a family of the poor is not credit-worthy will have to give place to the concept that many of the poor can be brought into the main stream of economic development through credit-worthy programmes". What is depressing is that, despite all these efforts, a considerable percentage of the population lives below the poverty line in India (Financial Express : 1990).

Since then, the financial institutions like CBS and RRBs have been asked to involve themselves actively in the implementation of various credit-based anti-poverty programmes like IRDP

ROLE OF BANKS IN IMPLEMENTING IRDP

The implementation of IRDP begins with the conduct of village survey by the grass-root level staff of BDOs Office. This survey helps to delineate the poor and the non-poor for IRDP assistance. All the applications are sent to District Rural Development Authority (DRDA) by the BDOs office for IRDP assistance. Later on, DRDA forwards eligible application forms to the concerned banks to advance loans. Then the financial institutions are not involved in the identification of beneficiaries, but they are asked to advance loans and to participate at the time of purchasing an asset to the beneficiary. Our field observations indicate that the mounting overdues under IRDP in the banks as reported by several bank managers was due to lack of co-operation and co-ordination between block and district level officials in recovering loans from the beneficiaries. The programme content also points out the importance of pre-inspection survey to be conducted by the concerned banks, to check whether the sanctioned scheme matches with the beneficiary's occupation. While identifying the beneficiaries, the staff members of the concerned bank are not involved; rather the DRDA selects the IRDP beneficiary based on the annual income of the poor household as assessed by the grass-root level official in the BDO's office. The eligible application forms shall be forward to the concerned banks by the DRDA. When once the purchase of the asset was over by the 'Purchasing Committee', then delinking between the bank, DRDA and BDO's office starts. For instance, our field observation reveals that a bamboo basket knitter was given a milch buffalo in Hosakote block of Bangalore District. The beneficiary reported that he had opted for IRDP assistance for basket knitting, but a dairy animal was sanctioned. This clearly show that the implementing agency did not take note of the beneficiary's characteristic futures and priority while sanctioning IRDP scheme. Hence, what is to be noted here is that the sanctioned scheme (a non-farm activity by nature) should match the beneficiary's own preference based on his occupation for generating additional income and employment. This may help in reducing the overdues in the banks.

COMPOSITION OF IRDP BENEFICIARIES

Let us look at the schemes sanctioned under IRDP by credit institutions. District-wise and bank-wise number of beneficiaries covered is given in Appendix - X. Of the 390 (200 old and 190 New) beneficiaries covered in the survey, CBs accounted for 69 per cent of the beneficiaries, while the rest were covered by RRBs. Kurian's (1987) study also pointed out more or less a similar trend when the survey data was analysed at the national level for the same period. The broad category of schemes is given in Appendix - XI. It can be seen that the beneficiaries under the schemes related to agriculture and dairy occupy a larger proportion (60 per cent) of the total beneficiaries. However, the economic base of the IRDP beneficiaries covered by CBs and RRBs differ substantially. In other words, a majority of the beneficiaries (69 per cent) covered by CBs were sanctioned loans for land linked schemes (Table 6.1); whereas, RRBs financed mostly for non-agricultural activities (44 per cent). The fact that emerges out of this is that rural diversification can be possible by involving RRBs through IRDP schemes. An analysis of IRDP schemes across caste-cum-occupation-based household industries, viz., wool-weaving, pottery and services (dhobi, barber, cobbler) revealed that these schemes can be strengthened through upgrading the existing technology like skill formation, assured demand for the produce (implies marketing and infrastructure facilities) and sizeable loans. A similar view was expressed in the

Table 6.1 : IRDP Schemes by Type of Banks

Scheme	Financial Institutions				Combined	% to Total
	CBs	% to total	RRBs	% to total		
Agriculture	48	18	16	13	64	16
Dairy	137	51	35	29	172	44
Other Animal husbandry	29	11	16	13	45	12
Village Industries	8	3	19	16	27	7
Trading	39	14	28	23	67	17
Services	9	3	6	5	15	4
Total	**270**	**100**	**120**	**100**	**390**	**100**

CRAFICARD report that the weaker sections can be helped to participate in the main-stream of development process through credit coupled with the new technology (RBI, 1981). It implies that, lack of capital to make use of the available technology impedes the weaker sections from participating in the development process. Further, schemes covered by RRBs under trading, which include petty shop, cloth business and fish vending, account for 23 per cent.

Table 6.2 furnishes details about the mandays spent by the beneficiaries in visiting block office, bank, etc., for getting IRDP assistance. It elucidates that the majority of RRBs beneficiaries (i.e., 81 per cent) have spent less than 10 days, while only 68 per cent of CBs beneficiaries fall in this class interval. This could be attributed mainly to the location of the bank. By and large, the bulk of the beneficiaries (92 per cent) got IRDP assistance by spending less than 20 days (Table 6.2). Similarly, an attempt is also made to work out the amount of money spent by IRDP beneficiaries for receiving IRDP assistance. About 81 per cent and 68 per cent of

Table 6.2 : Number of Days Spent by Beneficiaries in Getting IRDP Assistance

No. of Days	CBs		RRBs		Combined	
	Average Days Spent	Total Days Spent	Average Days Spent	Total Days Spent	Average Days Spent	Total Days Spent
Below 10	8	184 (68)	5	97 (81)	6	281 (72)
10–20	16	59 (22)	12	17 (14)	15	76 (20)
20–30	25	14 (5)	21	5 (4)	23	19 (5)
30–40	34	8 (3)	30	1 (1)	32	9 (2)
40 +	40	5 (2)	--	--	40	5 (1)
Total	**14**	**270 (100)**	**7**	**120 (100)**	**10**	**390 (100)**

Note : Figures in brackets denotes percentage to total.

beneficiaries of RRBs and CBs, respectively, spent Rs.150/- to avail of the assistance. It is note-worthy here that there is an inverse relationship between RRB beneficiaries and CB beneficiaries in terms of the amount spent (Table 6.3) and the number of days spent (Table 6.2). The percentage variation could be again attributed to the distance of the bank to rural and weaker sections. The table also reveals that nearly 50 per cent of the RRBs beneficiaries and 25 per cent of CBs beneficiaries spent less than Rs.50 to get IRDP assistance.

Table 6.3 : Amount Spent by the Beneficiaries in Getting IRDP Assistance

Amount Spent (Rs.)	CBs		RRBs		Combined	
	Average amount Spent per hh.	Total amount Spent per hh.	Average amount Spent per hh.	Total amount Spent per hh.	Average amount Spent per hh.	Total amount Spent per hh.
Upto 50	45	63 (23)	33	55 (46)	40	118 (30)
51–100	89	26 (10)	68	11 (9)	79	37 (10)
101–150	138	85 (31)	124	33 (28)	132	118 (30)
151–200	182	34 (13)	161	14 (12)	172	48 (12)
201–250	240	29 (11)	218	4 (3)	230	33 (9)
251 +	266	33 (12)	255	3 (2)	261	36 (9)
Total	**143**	**270 (100)**	**90**	**120 (100)**	**126**	**390 (100)**

Note : Figures in brackets denotes percentage to total.

It can be seen from Table 6.4 that IRDP beneficiaries are classified, based on Economic category, by both CBs and RRBs. The significance of the economic category (Rao and Erappa : 1987) is to delineate the rural community under three heads viz., the bottom, middle and upper. The coverage of bottom and middle group comes to a little over 95 per cent in the case of RRBs, as compared to CBs (94 per cent). The leakages in terms of sanctioning of IRDP schemes to non-poor accounts for 5 to 6 per cent for the sample of 390 beneficiaries covered in Karnataka. The noteworthy feature that comes out from the Table is that the Anthyodaya approach which was followed has helped in covering the poorest among the poor (bottom group) who constitute 46 per cent of the total IRDP beneficiaries.

Table 6.4 : IRDP Beneficiaries by Economic Category and Types of Bank

Group	Type of Bank		Combined
	CBs	RRBs	
Bottom	128 (47.0)	51 (42.5)	179 (46.0)
Middle	127 (47.0)	63 (52.5)	189 (49.0)
Upper	15 (6.0)	6 (5.0)	21 (5.0)
Total	**270** **(100)**	**120** **(100)**	**390** **(100)**

Note : Figures in bracket are percentage to total

Table 6.5 furnishes the composition of old beneficiaries (who have availed of the scheme two years before the survey month) by economic categories as covered by CBs and RRBs. Under both types of banks, leakages i.e. upper group getting assistance,

Table 6.5 : Distribution of IRDP Beneficiaries (old) by Type of Bank and Economic Category

Group	CBs	RRBs	Combined
Bottom	73 (50)	16 (29)	89 (45)
Middle	65 (45)	36 (66)	101 (50)
Upper	7 (5)	3 (5)	10 (5)
Total	**145** **(100)**	55 (100)	200 (100)

Note : Figures in bracket are percentage to total

accounted for 5 per cent. The bottom group coverage seems to be more in the case of CBs than RRBs.

Table 6.6 shows that the overdues of IRDP beneficiaries were financed by the two financial institutions. It reveals that 31 per cent of the beneficiaries of RRBs have no overdues. Also, the proportion of beneficiaries having overdues of more than Rs.1,000 is higher for commercial banks (42 per cent) when compared to RRBs (31 per cent).

Table 6.6 : Overdues of IRDP Beneficiaries by Type of Bank

(Percentage)

Overdues (Rs.)	CBs	RRBs	Total
No Overdues	26	31	27
1–500	8	11	9
500–1000	24	27	25
1000+	42	31	39
Total	**100**	**100**	**100**
Actuals	**145**	**55**	**200**

Finally, one can take a look at the number of IRDP beneficiaries who crossed the so-called poverty line (i.e., Rs.3,500/-). Here also RRBs beneficiaries who crossed the poverty line are more in number (55 per cent) (Table 6.7). While, in the case of CBs, only 45 per cent of the beneficiaries moved above the poverty line. Also, across different schemes, in most of them, the proportion of beneficiaries crossing the poverty line is higher in the case of RRB's beneficiaries than that of the commercial banks' beneficiaries.

Table 6.7 : Number of IRDP Beneficiaries who Crossed Poverty Line by Type of Bank and Schemes

(Percentage)

Scheme	CBs	RRBs	Total
Agriculture	50	82	58
Other Animal Husbandry	42	58	45
Trading	50	40	47
Village Industries	--	70	14
Services Class	100	25	40
Actuals	**65**	**29**	**94**
% to total	**45**	**53**	**47**

CONCLUSION

The co-ordinated efforts of financial institutions are essential along with other agencies to implement effectively the anti-poverty programmes. Though rural branches of CBs were increasing over a period of time, their accessibility to the poor did not increase in the same proportion. Based on this experience, separate rural financial institutions, popularly known as RRBs, came to be established. Since their inception, there was a tremendous expansion both in their number and branches in rural areas. The efficiency of delivery of assistance under IRDP and also the impact of the programme in terms of retention of assets, income generation, repayment of loan, crossing of poverty line, the performance of RRBs seem to be relatively better than those of commercial banks. Now, the basic question is, can these results have anything to do with the location of the Bank? Or is it also due to the staff members of RRBs who would have established close contacts with the beneficiaries because of their nearness? If it is so, can RRBs shoulder the responsibility of implementation of anti-poverty programmes exclusively? The clue that emerges from Karnataka's experience is that Regional Rural Banks seem to be better suited for implementation of the Integrated Rural Development Programme.

7

Revisit and Case Studies

This chapter deals with the analysis on expost situation of IRDP beneficiaries who took loan seven years ago and it is hoped that such an analysis would help us to assess the levels of socio-economic transformation of the beneficiary households. To accomplish this, interviews were conducted with the same beneficiaries whom this researcher had surveyed as part of a study of the Concurrent Evaluation undetaken in 1985-86. For the purpose of the present study,the revisits were made after five years during September, October and November 1990. At the outset, this chapter presents the justification for the villages selected for this study. It examines the role of the financial institutions in recovering the loans and advancing the second loan. Then the chapter presents some cases of successful beneficiaries and failure cases. Finally it attempts to draw some inferences from the cases studied in respect of income and employment status.

The revisited blocks, villages and beneficaries in respective districts and zones are given in Chapter 3 (Table 3.3). The selection of four blocks (which represent two each of developed and backward blocks) and the villages is based on this researcher's own judgement. This procedure was adopted to understand the sustainability from the point of view of household and also IRDP programme itself across the zones. In other words, if what was expected at both levels (i.e., family and programme) is realised, or is not realised could be explained through identifying the characteristics either way. To what extent did the IRDP investments generate increased income and employment to the target group. On the one hand, the success of the programme could be attributed to the inherent capacity of the household to absorb the scheme sanctioned. On the other hand, the designing of the programme seems to be weak, which resulted in the non-intactness of the asset (sold or perished), its income and employment generation. The intention here is to examine the design of the programme in terms of its appropriateness from the point of view of the families' perception.

Generally, the levels of participation of the beneficiaries with the programme indicate the degree of success of the programme. For example, given the base / characteristics of the village and also the beneficiaries, very few succeed but others could not. In other words, the beneficiaries have to shoulder more responsibility than the supportive factors to promote the scheme for the sustenance. Given this background, this chapter also analyses the impact of government policies, such as, the introduction of Agricultural Debt Relief Scheme (for more details see chapter 3) to IRDP beneficiaries as implemented through financial institutions. The purpose of furnishing a few case studies is to identify the characteristic features of the village, scheme and beneficiary. This, perhaps, gives us some clues for questions like why certain schemes are promoted? under what conditions ? why a few beneficiaries' absorption capacity in crossing the poverty line seems to be significant despite inherent weakness at the household ? Certainly the success stories would have faced painful and bitter experiences but for the skills and entrepreneurial capabilities of the beneficiaries which resulted in positive trends. The poor perception of the beneficiaries and adverse attitude towards the programme, perhaps, end up as a failure case and vice-versa.

The IRDP beneficiaries whom we met during revisits at Hosakote and Sringeri blocks (These two are classified as developed blocks) coming under two different agro-climatic zones viz., Southern Dry Zone and Plantation Zone have been financed by the State Bank of Mysore. Whereas in the other two blocks i.e., Hangal and Haveri (these two are classified as backward blocks) the beneficiaries are served by the State Bank of India and Malaprabha

Gramena Bank respectively. These two blocks represent the characteristic features of the Transition Zone and The Northern Dry Zone.

The commercial banks in Hoskote had financed the IRDP beneficiaries just then. As per the ledger maintained by the bank, out of 10 selected beneficiaries, except 4, the other beneficiaries availed themselves of more than one form of assistance under IRDP. The first loan was advanced during 1983-84 and the second was being given in 1988/1989. None of the beneficiaries for whom schemes were sanctioned for the second time had received the asset. The beneficiaries were ignorant about the second assistance during revisit. One possibility is, that the second loan was sanctioned exactly a year ago by the bank anticipating the government debt relief scheme, which facilitated the bank officials to make book adjustment of advancing the loan and recovering the same. The government debt relief to waive the loans was introduced and implemented on 1st October, 1990. The benefit received by the IRDP beneficiaries under ADRS ranged between Rs.3,387 and Rs.10,000. By and large, the over-dues (both I and II assistance) of the beneficiaries were taken care of by ADRS and most of the accounts were closed in October 1990. The interest on the loan was charged upto October 1989.

The procedure followed to write-off the loans was by legal suit filed during 1988 and 1989 and the legal fee was credited to the beneficiaries account. The overdues include the loan amount (less of repayment made) plus interest on loans plus legal fees which was also deducted from the government relief amount. Such a policy had encouraged the wilful defaulters and had turned a blind eye (without giving any incentives) to those beneficiaries who helped in recycling of the money.

The procedure adopted in Bangalore (rural) district for implementing the government relief was as follows: The Deputy Commissioner convenes the District Consultative Committee meeting for banking development (under lead bank scheme) to discuss and declare *annawari** to implement the ADRS after assessing the

* Annewari means assessing the principal crop yield per acre which is less than 35 per cent to declare a particular village/taluk affected by drought. This is being declared by the concerned Deputy Commissioner / Assistant commissioner / Tahasildar of the district / division / taluka / village. This is applicable to agricultural purpose only.

percentage of average yield per acre, as per Crop Cutting experiments conducted by local revenue officials. The *annawari* was declared for 1985-86 to 1989-90 for the affected villages in the taluk. The criteria followed to declare *annawari* are : (1) if the crop yield is less than 35 per cent (2) the beneficiaries should be declared as insolvent in the court and (3) beneficiary should have expired. Such of those beneficiaries who had overdues in between 2nd October 1986 and 2nd October 1989 are eligible to avail of ADRS. The same procedure was followed in the other districts where this researcher visited.

The discussion we had with the concerned bank officials who financed IRDP loans revealed that the banks are not going to lose the loan amount because, these are protected by the Deposit Insurance Corporation under the Credit Guarantee Scheme (DICGC).* In case the bank did not get the loan amount back from the beneficiary, then the concerned bank claims it from the DICGC. As per the bank records, claims were made by the bank to DICGC (except 3 cases in Hoskote block) and the accounts were settled during 1989-90.

During revisits we could meet 40 beneficiaries of the total sample covered at the time of Concurrent Evaluation. Out of 40, 15 (38 per cent) had retained the original assets, 4 had partially retained (i.e., calf existing), while the other 21 had either sold or partially sold the assets due to diseases like *Gundiselya* (heart attack), dysentery, *kaluvodutha*, not potential for pregnency, fodder problem , drought condition, heavy rain and cold climatic condition which normally prevails in the plantation zone. Only a few beneficiaries had tried to contact the concerned local veterinary doctors. Consequently, very few animals survived, while others died either due to the late treatment or negligence. Some of the villages were not accessible to the veterinary dispensary staff this could be because of the lack of transport facilities and very bad condition of the roads.

The value of assets (mainly animal husbandry scheme) sold by the beneficiaries ranged from Rs.250 to Rs.4,400. In Hoskote

* The DICGC accepts insurance on IRDP loans by the concerned bank which has sanctioned the IRDP loan. If the bank did not get the loan amount back from the beneficiary, then the concerned bank claims it from the DICGC. In turn DICGC pays the loan amount to the bank. Therefore, in real terms, banks are not losing the loan amount sanctioned to the beneficiaries.

block a few beneficaries sold immediately and others within 3 years. A few beneficiaries also reported that the animals they received were quite old and did not generate sufficient income and could not last long. The life of the animal, however, seems to be around 16 years in the study area. While sanctioning the scheme, the age of the animal is important rather than covering insurance (IRDP manual 1988). In other words, the age of the asset particularly of the cattle, seems to be very important as it determines the potential to generate additional income to the household for a considerable period.

Table 7.1 furnishes the details of distribution of schemes, the average annual income generated and ICOR at two points of time i.e., 1985-86 and 1990-91 in revisited villages. The average annual income generated by the asset (those schemes generating income) schemes under ISB sector like trading (petty shop and fish vending) seems to be more than the income generated by schemes under agricultural activities and dairy. The increase in income, however, seems to be substantial, by and large, it is true with all the schemes as compared between 1985-86 and 1990-91. This was mainly because of multiplication of assets in the study area over a period of 7 years. The low income generation, perhaps, could be attributed to several reasons like death, sale, drought, lack of vetarinary services and fodder problem, especially in the case of sheep and goat units. Initially the income generated by the asset (sheep and goat) was considerable in the first point and declined during 1990-91 because, some of the animals were dead due to the chronic diseases which attacked them during 1986-87. However, the average income generated (per scheme) was higher in the case of animal husbandry than the others during Concurrent Evaluation, but non-farm activities picked up in 1990-91. The reason could be that income acceleration was continuous in non-farm activities, unlike the risk bearingness with other schemes. The purpose of computing ICOR for all the beneficiaries who availed of similar schemes is to know the extent of capital depletion.* Though income generated by the asset was more between 1985-86 and 1990-91, the decapitalisation of money was higher in the case of land-linked schemes than non-farm activities.

* Capital depletion means depletion / erosion of the asset created due to natural wear and tear or death of animal or sale of asset by the beneficiary.

Table 7.1 : Distribution of Schemes of IRDP Beneficiaries, Average Annual Income Generation and ICOR

Schemes	No. of Beneficiaries	Annual Income Generated by the Asset (per hhs.)		For all Beneficiaries (per hhs.)		ICOR			
						For those hhs. income Generated		*For all Households*	
		1985-86	1990-91	1985-86	1990-91	1985-86	1990-91	1985-86	1990-91
Dairy	24	1102 (12)	4651 (8)	551	1550	1.83	.70	5.28	1.88
Pair of Bullocks	8	1800 (3)	5167 (3)	675	2313	2.52	.46	4.48	1.31
Bullocks & Cart	4	2500 (1)	5500 (1)	500	1375	4.07	.91	9.35	3.40
Sheep/Goat	2	4000 (1)	1225 (2)	2000	1225	2.88	1.00	1.73	2.88
Trading	2	700 (2)	8250 (2)	700	8250	1.25	.18	2.14	.18
Total	**40**	**1370 (19)**	**5010 (16)**	**651**	**2004**	**2.40**	**.81**	**4.71**	**1.53**

Note : Figures in brackets are number observations generated income by the asset.
Source : Concurrent Evaluation Survey and Data generated from Revisits.

The ICOR was calculated for those beneficiaries whose asset had generated income and also to all the beneficiaires. Table 7.1 shows that the lower the ratio of ICOR (as in the case of trading activities) the higher will be the income generation per rupee investment and vice-versa. As compared between two points of time, 1990-91 ICOR figures show tremendous improvement over Concurrent Evaluation (1985-86) results. In other words, in the long-run (after 7 years),viability of the schemes is more visible (for those households where assets were retained) than the short-run (after 2 years) outcome of the IRDP in the study area.

Table 7.2 indicates the percentage of IRDP asset income to the total income of the household. The over-all picture of the schemes shows that after two years and after seven years, the contribution of IRDP assets remains the same (a little less than 30 per cent) and that from other source of income was significantly high. But across the schemes and over a period of time i.e., seven years,experience reveals mixed trends. While for schemes like dairy, sheep and goat one can notice a decline in the IRDP's share, for bullocks and cart and trading one can notice an increase in the same. Nevertheless, there are individual cases where the income generated by IRDP assets accounts for more than 80 per cent. This type of result can be seen in all the schemes.

Table 7.2 : Income from IRDP Schemes and Other Source of Income

(Percentage)

Scheme	After Two Years		After Seven Years	
	Asset	Other Sources	Asset	Other Sources
Dairy	40	60	35	65
Pair of Bullocks	24	76	10	90
Bullocks & Cart	20	80	26	74
Sheep/Goat	22	78	13	87
Trading	26	74	65	35
Total	**28**	**72**	**29**	**71**

An analysis is made to examine the income mobility / crossing the poverty line of IRDP beneficiaries in Table 7.3 based on the initial income. During or before 1983-84, all the beneficiaries

Table 7.3 : The Income Mobility of IRDP Beneficiaries in Karntaka

Income Group (Initial Annual Income)	1983-84	1985-86	1990-91
0 - 2265	28	4	1
2266 - 3500	11	15	7
3501 - 4800	1	11	5
4801 - 6400	--	7	--
6400 - 10500	--	2	13
10500 +	--	1	14
Total	**40**	**40**	**40**

(except 1) were below the poverty line i.e., Rs.3,500. During Concurrent Evaluation except 10 per cent of the total destitutes households, the others had moved to the next income groups. It is established from Table 7.3 that the probability of crossing the poverty line is more, not only to those whose initial income was close to the poverty line but also to the poorest of the poor. This could be attributed to the big push factor for such of those households which availed of non-farm schemes.

Between 1985-86 and 1990-91, out of 40 beneficiaries, about 3 and 27 beneficiaries crossed the official poverty line i.e., Rs.6,400 respectively. It is interesting to note here that, except 32 per cent, all other beneficiaries reached / crossed the poverty line during 1990-91 (Table 7.3).

The extent of debt relief under ARDS availed of by the beneficiaries across the schemes and agro-climatic zones is indicated in Table 7.4. The interesting feature here is that, though schemes coming under trading activity (which are non-agriculture) are not entitled to avail of debt relief benefits, they have voluntarily cleared the loans within (the stipulated period) two years. The beneficiaries in the developed blocks availed of ARDS higher than in the backward blocks. Among the schemes, the dairy scheme got more debt relief money than the other schemes across the zones (Table 7.4).

Table 7.4 : Debt Relief Per IRDP Beneficiaries in Karnataka

Scheme/Zone	SDZ	NDZ	TZ	PZ	Total
Dairy	5896 (9)	2243 (4)	1363 (4)	--	3970 (17)
Pair of Bullocks	--	2736 (2)	2492 (2)	1305 (1)	2352 (5)
Bullocks & Cart	--	1712 (2)	--	5356 (2)	3534 (4)
Sheep/Goat	--	2300 (1)	1767 (1)	--	2034 (2)
Trading	--	--	--	--	--
Total	**5896 (9)**	**2241 (9)**	**1743 (7)**	**4006 (3)**	**3434 (28)**

Note : Figures in the brackets denote the number of observations.

A FEW CASE STUDIES

In the following, an attempt is made to study a few cases of those who belong to different caste groups and have availed of different schemes, by examining their family background and also the village base to identify the characteristics as to how these households have been able to over-come the poverty syndrome. Not all IRDP beneficiaries sustain permanently, except very few. Why is it that only a few cases succeed and others cannot? These aspects of rural poverty are being carefully examined in this section. What are the variables (economic, social, cultural and education) responsible for the rural poor to over-come the vicious circle of poverty? Is it confined to region specific or a particular group/ groups. To understand a problem like rural poverty,perhaps, one has to look into various dimensions in which the rural poor live.

CASE 1

Dodda Muniyappa, 45 years, belonging to Scheduled Caste (a *holaya*) is an inhabitant of Sonnallipura in Hosakote Taluk. He lives with his fellow caste men in a separate portion of the village called *Harijan* Colony, which is the common feature of most of the villages in Karnataka and in India too. The village is situated in the semi-irrigated area of the taluk.

The above case was a nuclear family* living in a house with mud walls and tiled roof, which was availed of under the *Janatha* Housing Scheme—a Government Programme. He was a marginal farmer, having two acres of land which he got under the surplus land distribution programme, as reported during the concurrent evaluation and the same is retained even at the time of revisit. Though it was a land-owning household, it pursued *coolie* as a main occupation and agriculture as subsidiary before availing of IRDP.

A milch cow (Heiefer) worth Rs.4,000 was sanctioned to him in 1983. The asset was retained only for one year and sold for Rs.3,000 thereafter. However, during the first year the asset generated income upto Rs.800. The milk was supplied to the Milk Co-operative Society which was already existing in the village before IRDP could reach the households/village.

Though this beneficiary had not crossed the poverty line (Rs.3,500) even after two years, his annual income was reported to have reached the cut off point of the poverty line. Exactly one year before ARDS was implemented during October 1990, as per the bank records, one more milch cow, worth about Rs.4,375 was sanctioned to him. The Beneficiary reported that he was neither aware of the second loan sanctioned nor had he received the milch animal. But under ARDS, he got Rs.8,500 and thereby, the first loan and the second loan over-dues of Rs.4,200 and Rs.4,375 respectively, were deducted and both accounts closed in October 1990 by the concerned bank, wihtout the knowledge of the beneficiary.

Interestingly, Dodda Muniyappa possessed the skill of rearing silk-worms. Though he does not grow mulberry, he rears silk worms by purchasing mulberry leaf from others. He reared 50 disease free layings (dfls) in his residence and harvested 15 to 20 kgs of cocoons on an average per crop. He harvested 3 to 4 times in a year and earned an income of Rs.3,500 to Rs.4,000 (per year/ crop).

It may be noted here that, a part of the income generated by the IRDP asset (when the asset was with him) was spent on his

* "The nuclear family consists typically of a married man and woman with their offspring although in individual cases one or more additional persons may reside with them" (Murdock's definition quoted by Shah : 1973).

children's education to meet the expenditure of his two sons who are studying in second year B.A. and 8th Standard, respectively. Now, he is depending on the additional income generated by silk-worm rearing for his children's education.

CASE 2

Anjanamma, *Golla* by caste, aged about 45 years, lives with her husband and 5 children (one daughter and four sons) in Kamblipura of Hoskote Taluk. The family owns ancestral property of 1.5 acres of dry land and a *semi pucca* house (mud walls with tile roof). *Ragi*, a millet crop, is grown for household consumption. The yield, as reported by her, seems to be low and is attributed to the scanty rainfall. They faced several problems (like scarcity of food and clothing) and on some occasions went without food during drought years. Under these circumstances, Anjanamma got a hybrid cow, under IRDP programme, worth Rs.4,000 in 1983-84. Though she owned some land, she declared her main occupation as *coolie* (labourer) for availing of IRDP loan. But availing of IRDP loan has helped the family to improve its economic status by selling milk. Only when the family is free from dairy activity, it could go for coolie. Thus, milk enterprise became the primary occupation of the household. The socio-economic status of the household improved significantly, due to the additional income and employment generated by the asset.

At the time of concurrent evaluation, this beneficiary repaid Rs.925/- and the rest of the loan amount was cleared in the successive years, as reported by the respondent. But, as per the bank ledger, the over-dues of the loan amount +interest of Rs.3,714 were written-off by closing the account in 1990, due to the implmenetation of the governments' debt relief scheme.

Despite the drought condition that prevailed during 1983, 1984 and 1985, while other beneficiaries sold their assets, she retained them and struggled hard and managed to get the feed and fodder which she brought from the neighbouring villages. The retention of the asset, however, was attributed to the collective attitude of the family members. Otherwise,the asset should have been sold away along with the assets of the other beneficiaries.

The cow gave birth to eight calves (three female and five male). All male calves were sold for Rs.400 at the rate of Rs.80 per calf within one week of the birth,anticipating the milk yield will be less. Further, one cow was sold for Rs.5,000. Now the beneficiary is having three cows of which two are giving milk around 25 liters per day. The multiplication of calves took place within the gestation period of 5 to 7 months in a year. In 1986-87 Kamblipura had its own Milk Co-operative Society which reduced the drudgery of the beneficiarys' husband of carrying the milk containers by bicycle to the nearby village milk society. It is noteworthy here that the role of an institution like milk society becomes essential to promote dairy activities. The milk was purchased by the society at the rate of Rs.5 per litre. The beneficiary used to get Rs. 1,500 to 2,000 per month after deduction against the feeds supplied by the milk society.

As a result of the additional income generated by the assets, the following changes have taken place in the beneficiary's household. Firstly, all the children of the household could avail of education in schools and colleges. It is interesting to note here that the children are also participating (collecting green fodder) in the maintenance of the assets. Secondly, the respondent purchased a house for Rs.8,000. Thirdly, Rs.12,000 was advanced to purchase two acres of land in the same village. The beneficiary intends to go for a borewell next year. Fourthly, they celebrated their daughter's marriage two years ago and spent nearly Rs.20,000. Fifthly, they have purchased consumer durables like almirah, wall clock, bicycle and wrist watches, and lastly, the annual income of the beneficiary,before the scheme (during 1983-84) as per record,was Rs.2,250 and it has been cumulatively multiplied to Rs.25,750 (from asset Rs.21,000 and Rs.4750 from other sources) in 1990. The beneficiary continued to sustain the programme and also move above the official poverty line of Rs.6,400 on a permanent basis. All these changes were possible because of the additional income generated by the asset. The inference that emerges from the experience of this household is that the level of participation in the programme and the collective attitude of the family members helped the transformation. This is inspite of droughts that prevailed in the past. The momentum in terms of increase in annual income picked up after the establishment of the milk co-operative society in the village. The rural transformation can be witnessed through the existence of the milk co-operative society.

CASE 3

Veerabhadrappa, 50 years old belonging to a dominant caste (lingayat), is a marginal farmer-cum-agricultural labourer in Hombardi village of Haveri Taluk in Dharwad District. His is a nuclear family of five members living in a thatched house with mud walls in the centre of the village. He was a marginal farmer having 1.2 acres of inherited dry land. Though the respondent is illiterate, he made all efforts to educate his two sons and a daughter upto the sixth, seventh and ninth standards, respectively,and later on they discontinued their studies due to financial problems.

Normally, jowar and tur crops are grown in his field. The yield of these crops depends on the vagaries of monsoon. The income earned from agriculture was not enough to make a living. Though it was a land-owning household, they hired out manual labour, as the earnings from agriculture were not sufficient to make both ends meet.

At this juncture, the respondent received a milch animal (she-buffalo) under IRDP in 1983. The asset was sold for Rs.800 exactly after one year because of the fodder problem prevailing due to drought. The beneficiary reported that the intensity of drought continued in the successive years also. Under these circumstances, along with other marginal farmers/agricultural labourers families in the village, he migrated to Raichur District where the canal work was on. They spent two years there and returned to the village. With whatever they could save they renovated their house. They also performed their daughter's marriage with some additional borrowings in the village.

Similar to that of crop-sharing system, *saripalu* (cattle share i.e., they rear others' cow/buffalo calf and when it gives birth, the calf is retained by the one who reared it. Once the lactation period is over, the milch animal has to be given back to the owner. Both (the rearer and the owner) share the milk daily. This system exists in most of the villages in Karnataka. This way he got a calf and he has become the owner of the cow. That cow gives five litres of milk per day and he earns Rs.675 per month. The annual income increased further due to good agriculture in a year and fetched him Rs.2,000.

Out of the total loan of Rs.2,000 he has repaid only Rs.356 and benefited under the debt relief scheme to the extent of Rs.2,680 and finally the account was closed in October 1990. Though he was unable to retain the IRDP asset due to obvious reasons, still his attitude towards rearing milch animal seems to be evident from the above experience.

CASE 4

Bassappa Nelogol, a resident of Chikkalingadahalli in Haveri Taluk, aged about 35 years, belongs to Kuruba caste. He had a big family consisting of seven members. The respondent inherited six acres of dry land and a house. Though he is a little above the cut-off point, i.e., the poverty line, to avail of IRDP he became eligible under land classification (IRDP manual : 1988) in northern Karnataka. The main occupation of the family is agriculture and sheep rearing is subsidiary.

Before availing of IRDP, he already had 10 sheep. Again, the respondent got 10 sheep and a ram under IRDP during 1983. The beneficiary was given 10 sheep and a ram worth Rs.4,000 by a Regional Rural Bank. Despite the multiplication of sheep, about 10 sheep died due to chronic disease and a few (ten) were sold for Rs.3,000 due to severity of drought. At the time of Concurrent Evaluation, the assets generated income upto Rs.1,200. At present, he owns 15 sheep. Because of this scheme their economic condition and social status have improved. Out of the income generated by the sheep unit, together with the income from agriculture, the beneficiary performed the marriages of his three daughters and spent Rs.15,000 each. The respondent repaid Rs.1,564 and also closed the account after availing of debt relief of Rs.2,300 in October 1990. None of the beneficaries received second dosage because, the first loan was not cleared. Due to demarcation of the area covered by the respective financial institution, now his village comes under the jurisdiction of the Corporation Bank which is located in a near-by village. The beneficiary intends taking one more IRDP loan for further extension of sheep rearing activity. His income from other sources, however, seems to be more than 60%, as reported during the revisiting time. The attitude of the beneficiary and also of the family members to participate in the development process in continuing with IRDP programme brought several changes at the household level.

CASE 5

Nadaf, a muslim is having a joint family* of 15 members living in the heart of the village. Except for two adults, all other members of the family are educated upto SSLC. The household owned 35 acres of land, (20 acres inherited land and 15 acres of land purchased during 1985-86), with three irrigation borewells. Unlike other cases, it was mainly an agricultural family (owned some agricultural implements like iron plough, two bullocks, a bullock cart and has now purchased one tractor, which is necessary for a self-sufficient agriculturist). No doubt, he is one of the large farmers in the village. He was also a member of the local panchayat at the time of availing of IRDP benefit. The land was divided among the family members just to avail of IRDP benefit i.e., a pair of bullocks during 1983. By listening to this during our revisit, a co-villager felt surprised to know this. This person got an IRDP loan at a time when Gramasabha Meetings were not conducted. Even before IRDP, he already had a pair of bullocks. The beneficiary sold the bullocks got under IRDP due to old age for Rs.6,000 (scheme amount was Rs.4,000) after four years and purchased a new pair for Rs.7,500.

The crops grown by this household are cotton, jowar, chillies, and brinjal. Apart from this, they also own a coconut garden. There is no doubt that, if we assess the annual income of the family, it will be around Rs.three lakhs from agricultural source. The beneficiary reported that the property was divided on record during 1989-90 and to his share he got 9 acres and an irrigation borewell. He grows commercial crops which fetch in Rs.1.5 lakhs.

CASE 6

J. K. Poojar, aged about 52, belonging to a dominant caste, is a large farmer and an IRDP beneficiary from Kondoji village in Hanagal Taluk. He is the head of the household of a collateral joint family with 17 members. The family owned 20 acres of land (8 acres irrigated and the rest dry land) and a *pucca* house having electricity. Further, he runs a petty shop. There is no surprise if we call the householder one of the large farmers in the village. Similar to Nadafs case, the land was divided among the brothers (6

---

* Joint family means two or more elementary families joined together. The above family belongs to patrilineal joint family because it is based on the principle of patrilineal descent (A M Shah : 1973).

in number) and availed of IRDP (a pair of bullocks) in 1983. Before IRDP scheme, he had already owned a pair of bullocks. Indeed, this household has not been benefited from ARDS, but it has availed of the subsidiary amount of IRDP scheme. The loan amount was cleared within the stipulated time and availed of further loans like crop loan and again a pair of bullocks during successive years. These loans are also cleared by the beneficiary. The IRDP bullocks were sold (due to old age) for Rs.4,000 and a younger one was purchased for Rs.6,800 during 1986-87. The bullocks were used for cultivation as well as transportation of manure to their lands. The prevailing hiring out rate of bullocks for agricultural purposes per day was Rs.50 in the village. If we compute the annual income generated by the asset (assuming six months work), it comes to around Rs.6,000. During 1986-87 the beneficiary availed of one more loan of IRDP to purchase a bullock cart and also a gobar gas plant for Rs.10,000. These loans were also voluntarily cleared within the prescribed period. During 1989-90, with the help of the Primary Land Development Bank, the respondent availed of a loan for irrigation borewells. During the same period, the State Bank of India also financed for a tractor. The tractor generates (hiring out) about Rs.3,000 to 4,000 per month. The annual income of the household (all sources) goes up to three lakhs. The above two cases reveal that the IRDP benefits were misutilised by the non-poor, who are socially and economically dominant in rural Karnataka.

CASE 7

Surappa is around 40 and is Vokkaliga by caste. He has one son and two daughters, besides his wife and his parents. During concurrent evaluation survey his occupation was that of running a petty shop. He owns one acre of land and grows paddy crop and arecanut. Due to financial constraints the petty shop was closed in 1982. In 1983 he availed of the benefit of the ISB scheme (for petty shop) worth Rs.2,000. The loan amount plus interest was cleared within the stipulated time i.e., in 1984, before the first visit. He expressed his disappointment at not being given the second dosage under IRDP, despite his promptness in repaying the loan. The reason given was that he doesn't belong to the power group in the village. But he suggested that for the success of the programme, constant monitoring of the scheme, at least by the local officials who are working at the grassroot level, should be there. Otherwise, the intactness of the asset and income and employment generation, perhaps, will be jeopardised.

CASE 8

Kantha, in his early 50s, lives in Vykuntapura of Sringeri block in Chikkamangalore district. He belongs to *bestha* (fisherman) community and is pursuing his traditional occupation of catching fish and trading in near-by villages and towns. The respondent's income has been assessed by the investigator during Concurrent Evaluation to be not sufficient to the family members to make both ends meet. He was happy at the time of revisit because, the scheme of fish vending, availed of in 1983, made him flourish. He has repaid the loan amount plus interest within the stipulated time out of the income generated by the scheme. The additional income and employment generated enabled him to purchase two acres of land (earlier he was landless) and also some urban made consumer durables. Further, he renovated his old house. The incremental capital output ratio seems to be highly significant i.e., .13. Interestingly he sent his two sons and a daughter to school and was also capable of providing school uniform, books etc., to the children. Further, he reported that expenditure on health was also taken care of by the IRDP income.

CASE 9

Bellanna Gowda, a resident of Kochavally, availed of a pair of bullocks under IRDP. He had two sons, besides his wife. The respondent is no more. His son Gopal, aged about 35 years, lives with his brother. They own one acre of land and a tiled roof house which is common in the plantation zone. They grow paddy crop and arecanut in their fields. Their main occupation is coolie. Initially,the IRDP assets generated income (and employment) of about Rs.1,500 annually for 2 years. The Bullocks died after two years due to disease called *Kaluodatha*. The beneficiary's sons reported that the bullocks given were aged and could not withstand the cold climatic condition of the region. In the plantation zone the rainfall normally will be more than 2,000mm. The bullocks cannot survive in that environment. The middle-men and the power group seem to be dominant in this zone. They tried to contact the local veterinary doctor to attend to the disease of the IRDP asset, but in vain. They expressed their dissatification over monitoring of IRDP by the concerned officials. They reported that none of the officials cooperated to claim insurance and this made them not to go and ask for further loan.

CONCLUSION

For a better understanding of the point of view of sustenance of the IRDP and also the beneficiaries' perceptions, we undertook revisits (1990-91) of the few villages where we had earlier conducted the Concurrent Evaluation (1985-86). The purpose here is to assess the direction of transformation across the schemes, blocks, zones and among the social groups over a period of time.

We have purposely selected 2 developed blocks and 2 backward blocks, covering 40 beneficiaries, representing 4 agro-climatic conditions in Karnataka (Table 1). By and large, those IRDP beneficiaries who availed of loans based on land-linked schemes were benefited from the ADRS introduced by the Central Government during 1990. However, there are a few cases where the beneficiaries themselves voluntarily cleared the IRDP loans. Interestingly, some of them were the poorest of the poor. Despite non-farm schemes of IRDP not coming under the purview of ADRS, their beneficiaries also had voluntarily closed the accounts within the stipulated time.

Further, the acceptance level of the non-farm schemes was highly significant in terms of generating income and employment. In other words, the sustenance of those schemes and also family perception go hand in hand making the poor households viable even in the long-run.

The implementation of ADRS by the banks functioning in those blocks seemed to be biased towards the better-off section among the target groups. In other words, the relief amount received by the upper group of the rural poor was more than that received by the poorest of the poor. Further, the relief money given under ARDS does not show any consistency across the scheme, among the social groups in the study area. The worst part of ADRS was that it showed a negative treatment to the prompt beneficiaries (voluntarily repaid the loans or some repayment was made) and encouraged totally the wilful defaulters by sanctioning ADRS money to clear the overdues.

While assessing the IRDP impact, the changes that have occurred in the rural poor households (here cases examined) reveal a different dimension to delve further deep in understanding the different facets of anti-poverty programmes on the one hand and amelioration of the rural poor on the other. For instance, very few beneficiaries retained IRDP assets (animal husbandry schemes) despite droughts, while others under agro-climatic stress disposed of the assets because of fodder problem. Non-retention of asset (particularly milch cows) was, however, attributed to the chronic diseases and also poor extension services of the local veterinary staff. The age of the animal and also the local climatic conditions were poorly being considered by the implementing agency at the grassroots level. Within the given rural system, in spite of the efficiency of the local bureaucracy and banks staff, the non-poor like Hemanna (Hosakote block), Nadaf and Gundappanavar (Haveri block), J K Poojar (Hangal block) and Srinivas (Sringeri block) etc., could not be prevented from getting the benefit of the IRDP programme. They have not only availed of IRDP loans but also reaped the fruits of ADRS. In other words, the benefits from most of the development programmes have been derived by the non-poor rather than by the deserving ones.

No doubt, IRDP has helped the beneficiaries from different walks of life. For example, the beneficiaries (here the poorest of the poor) are able to perform their daughter's marriage a little beyond their capacities, constructed a new house or effected alteration to the old house, advanced money for purchase of land, children got an opportunity to attend schools, purchased consumer durables and by and large improved their socio-economic condition through additional income and employment generated under IRDP schemes. Otherwise, the life of the entire family would have been miserable.

With some modification in the content of the IRD programme, perhaps, it may deliver the goods that it aimed at, in achieving the objectives like social justice, equity, and development. For instance, though the beneficiaries like Veerabhadrappa at Hombareddy Village in Haveri Block and Narayanappa at Kamblipura in Hosakote block were inclined to have assets (cattle), because of drought and debt (borrowed from the local money lender) they had to dispose them off. This could have been avoided if the implementing agency had provided working capital to meet the fodder expenses during the drought conditions.

8

Summary and Conclusions

Poverty exists either in its relative form which is predominantly seen in the developed countries, or in an absolute form as it prevails in the developing and under-developed countries. While the former is tolerable, the latter is most vulnerable, since a particular section of the society does not command the goods and services because of not having the economic wherewithal, though they are entitled to have them. This section of the people is called by different nomenclature like weaker sections, vulnerable group, target group, rural poor.

Anti-poverty programmes have been incorporated (though very marginally) in the Indian planning process since Independence. Community Development Programmes, down to Integrated Rural Development Programme (IRDP) and Jawahar Rozgar Yojana (JRY) are being implemented in the country. From time to time, these programmes are being conceived with modifications. In the beginning, the policy makers thought that developing the agricultural sector and achieving high growth rates in the economy would take care of the problem of poverty. The general failure of such a strategy to eradicate poverty has led to the adoption of direct attack programmes like IRDP.

IRDP is a major anti-poverty programme devised to alleviate rural poverty in India through direct attack. IRDP was launched in

1977-78 and initially, it covered 16 selected districts in the country. Later on, by 2nd October 1980 it was extended to all the 5011 administrative blocks in the country. The prime objective of IRDP is to identify the target group to provide them with productive assets and skills which help in generating additional income and employment opportunities and in turn, helping them to cross the official poverty line. The main thrust of IRDP is to utilise locally available resources and aim at integration of the sectoral programmes, to achieve growth and eradicate poverty and unemployment of the rural poor.

The implementation of the anti-poverty programmes like IRDP in India provides an interesting ground for undertaking research to find out the type of rural transformation that has taken place as a result of these special programmes. In fact, one of the ways to unfold the complexities of development processes is to understand the impact of some of the developmental programmes which are expected to transform the living conditions of the poorer sections of the population. For this, one has not only to analyse the content of the special programmes, but also look at these programmes from the point of view of the beneficiaries. Further, one may have to study and analyse a number of economic and non-economic factors which are at work to bring about the desired rural transformation through various anti-poverty programmes.

The review of literature attempted in the study on the implementation of IRDP revealed that a credit-based poverty alleviation programme like IRDP has been able to reach a large number of rural poor and thereby enabling them to acquire productive assets. However, a bulk of the households have not been able to sustain the activities taken up with IRDP assistance as they have either misutilised the funds or the assets have got decapitalised for other reasons. Though the scheme could increase the overall incomes, particularly of the poor, the increase has neither been substantial nor sustainable. As a result, IRDP has not been able to achieve its main objective of alleviating rural poverty and lift the rural poor permanently above the poverty line.

At the same time, the review of literature also helped in identifying a number of weaknesses in the implementation of these programmes. These are : inclusion of non-poor in the beneficiary group, lack of adequate forward and backward linkages, lack of awareness of the anti-poverty programmes on the part of the poorest of the poor, leakages through middle-men and inefficient bureaucracy.

Though the studies reviewed above have examined various issues connected with IRDP, they have not been able to analyse properly the socio-economic setting under which the IRDP has been operating. At the same time, the role played by various institutions, particularly institutional credit agencies which play a crucial role in implementing programmes like IRDP, has not been brought out clearly. Not many studies, therefore, have attempted to study IRDP from a holistic angle. Besides, almost all studies have done only one point evaluation of the scheme which fails to bring out clearly the sustainability of the scheme as well as its impact.

To understand the impact of IRDP,it is necessary to examine these issues more carefully. In order to fulfil this, the present study has been undertaken with special reference to Karnataka.

The objectives of this study are :

1. To assess the role of state intervention in alleviating rural poverty in Karnataka.
2. To analyse the impact of IRDP on socio-economic conditions of the beneficiaries.
3. To examine the role of financial institutions like Commercial Banks (CBs) and Regional Rural Banks (RRBs) in implementing IRDP.
4. To examine various policy alternatives for better implementation of poverty alleviation programmes.

DATA BASE / METHODOLOGY

This study is based on both secondary and primary sources of data. The secondary data was collected from various reports of the rural development department and Plan documents. The primary data for the study has been drawn from the Concurrent Evaluation Survey (CES) on IRDP conducted by the Institute for Social and Economic Change (ISEC) Bangalore between October 1985 and September 1986. The CES covered 40 villages in 20 blocks in 10 districts of Karnataka. With 390 beneficiaries who were selected on the basis of simple random sampling technique. The CES data was supplemented by this researcher's field work which collected information/data through schedules viz., Village Schedule, Household Schedule and Schedule for collecting Bank data.

Further, revisiting of villages was also undertaken after five years i.e. during 1990-91. Between the time of receiving assistance by beneficiaries (1983-84) and the writing of the thesis (1990-91), there was a gap of nearly seven years. During this period it is natural that certain changes would have taken place, not only in socio-economic conditions of the beneficiaries but also in their perceptions to the problem of poverty and poverty alleviation programmes. Also, with the lapse of time the issue of sustainability of the poverty alleviation schemes and their benefits also become important. Hence, a need was felt for updating the information on socio-economic dynamics of the beneficiaries' households. It was, therefore, decided to conduct a revisit covering 40 beneficiaries (out of 200 old beneficiaries covered in CES), spread over 8 villages in 2 developed and 2 backward blocks. At the time of revisits, apart from canvassing a brief structured schedule, conversational interviews were also held with the beneficiaries, bank officials and elders (other than IRDP beneficiaries in those villages). The collected data has been analysed descriptively by using percentages, averages and ratios and by calculating the Incremental Capital Output Ratio (ICOR) to assess the impact of IRDP. Case studies of a few IRDP beneficiaries have also been attempted to assess its impact.

MAJOR FINDINGS

By and large, the physical and financial achievements were higher than the target set in all the districts in implementing IRDP in Karnataka. It may be noted that a higher per capita investment was made on IRDP beneficiaries during the beginning of the Sixth and Seventh Plans across the districts in the State. The percentage of SC/ST beneficiaries to total beneficiaries coverage was 26 per cent, which is less than the government norm of 30 per cent. However, the coverage of SC/ST beneficiaries to total has increased over the years.

The socio-economic-demographic characteristics of IRDP households reveal the following : In the initial period of IRDP implementation, there appears to be gender bias (only 10 per cent of women beneficiaries covered to total beneficiaries). The beneficiaries' age was not taken into consideration (60 per cent of them had crossed 40 years of age) while sanctioning the scheme. More than 70 per cent of the households had five members in the family, and 67 per cent had two earning members, mostly engaged as *coolie* (manual labourers). Further, more than 52 per cent of the households had 3 or more dependents in the study area. And most of the dependents are in the age group 0 - 14.

Nearly 80 per cent of the households belonged to the illiterate category. About 46 per cent of IRDP beneficiaries were neither owning land nor cultivating land. Though a few identified beneficiaries (mostly in Northern Dry Zone) had more than five acres of land, still they were eligible (under land classification in those districts) to avail of IRDP assistance. Around 17 per cent and 2 per cent of the beneficiaries had non-farm activities as their main occupation in backward blocks and developed blocks, respectively.

Around 88 per cent of the selected villages did not have veterinary services, but were located at a distance of more than 5 kms. Marketing of IRDP assets products (except milk in Southern Dry Zone villages) seems to be very weak because, the market places and nearby towns are far away from these villages. The credit institutions (except 20 per cent of the villages) are away (more than 5 kms) from the selected villages. Many villages are drought-prone. The marginal farmers and agricultural labourers migrate to nearby places for wage employment during droughts.

In the initial stage of implementation of IRDP, the implementing agency did not give due coverage for women beneficiaries in Karnataka. The schemes that were sanctioned for women beneficiaries are dominated by dairy and trading activities. 87 per cent of the schemes sanctioned for women beneficiaries were concentrated in developed blocks and only the rest in the backward blocks. Dairy schemes are more popular with women beneficiaries. The number of women beneficiaries covered and the schemes sanctioned under ISB sector show a increasing trend since 1984-85 in the State. In other words, non-farm activities are picking up in rural Karnataka under IRDP. However, there is little difference between men and women beneficiaries so far as overdues are concerned.

The distribution of land-linked schemes is found more in developed blocks and non-land based schemes are relatively more in backward blocks. It may be pointed out here that in the case of backward blocks, the major constraint is the marketing of the products made by the village craftsmen.

Better performance by the bottom group in terms of their timely repayment of loans helped in recycling of credit. This has been possible because of income generation by the IRDP assets of bottom group beneficiaries. The percentage of income generated by the asset to the total annual income was much higher in the case of bottom group beneficiaries and vice versa in the case of the other groups. The number of middle and upper group beneficiaries in crossing the poverty line was more than the number belonging to the bottom group beneficiaries.

For certain schemes there is need to bypass the criteria of agro-climatic base of zones. For example, schemes like dairying have been successfully implemented in all the zones. Consequently many villages have milk co-operatives due to IRDP.

The Incremental Capital Output Ratio (ICOR) of all the schemes was 2.92. Across the blocks, the productivity was higher in the backward blocks (2.61) than in the developed blocks (4.31). The higher productivity is because of the non-farm schemes sanctioned in backward blocks which generated more income. The schemes under agricultural activities showed relatively lower profitability than non-farm activities. Across social groups, IRDP schemes seem to be more profitable for those in the higher caste groups. The ICOR in the case of higher income groups shows a lower ratio. Though the overall ICOR is fairly low, sharp variations could be found across zones, blocks, castes and income groups.

The beneficiaries who have availed of the schemes under village industries and services (40 out of 42) had continued to pursue their traditional household occupations (i.e. wool weaving, cobbler, washermen, carpenter, lime stone, brick-making).

The number of beneficiaries who crossed the poverty line (Rs.3,500) accounted for 48 per cent of the total beneficiaries who availed of schemes under IRDP in the State. However, it was also found that mainly those who were close to the poverty line before getting the assistance could cross it.

The analysis of the performance and the role of financial institutions like commercial banks and Regional Rural Banks in the implementation of IRDP reveals the following aspects:-

Commercial banks (CBs) financed more for land-linked schemes, while Regional Rural Banks (RRBs) financed schemes mostly for non-agricultural activities (village industries, trading etc.). Most of the beneficiaries (81 per cent) of RRBs spent less than 10 days in getting IRDP schemes, whereas 68 per cent of CBs beneficiaries fall in this group. About 55 per cent and 33 per cent of RRBs and CBs beneficiaries, respectively spent Rs.100 to avail of IRDP schemes in Karnataka.

The other dimension observed was that the staff members of RRBs were gradually establishing close contact with the beneficiaries. This is clearly revealed by the fact that 31 per cent of the RRBs beneficiaries had no overdues. The number of beneficiaries who crossed the poverty line (Rs.3,500) also is more in RRBs (55 per cent) as compared to CBs (45 per cent) beneficiaries under IRDP in the State. The RRBs thus seem to have implemented IRDP in a better way.

In addition to the above findings the following observations made during the revisits are listed here : (1) the non-farm schemes' acceptance level was highly significant in terms of generating income and employment, (2) very few beneficiaries (here cases examined) retained IRDP assets (animal husbandry schemes) despite droughts, while others under agro-climatic stress disposed of the assets because of fodder problem, chronic diseases and poor extension services of the local veterinary staff, (3) the age of the animal and the local climatic conditions were poorly being integrated by the implementing agency, (4) the living standards of the IRDP beneficiaries improved, as would be seen from the social cycle activities like daughters marriage, construction/alteration of the house, spending money to purchase land, children attending school and purchase of consumer durables, (5) By the implementation of the Agriculture Debt Relief Scheme (ADRS) to waive off overdues of IRDP beneficiaries, (except non-farm activities) the better off among the poor have benefited more than the deserving ones. The ADRS has facilitated the wilful defaulters more than the prompt repayers.

POLICY IMPLICATIONS

Based on the above findings,the following policy implications have been drawn with regard to implementation of IRDP :-

(1) The target group which comprises of small and marginal farmers, SC/STs, artisans and agricultural labourers is not homogeneous. Absence of efforts on the part of the implementing agencies to design programmes to suit the needs of a heterogeneous group has been one of the basic weaknesses of IRDP. Therefore, identifying the heterogeneity of the group and sanctioning schemes accordingly would make sense and would also facilitate faster economic transformation of the rural poor households.

(2) In addition to identifying the heterogeneity of the target groups, the implementing agency should design programmes which will take care of the regional variations. This requires knowledge of rural areas and the potentialities of these areas for pursuing certain activities. At present, irrespective of the regional peculiarities, schemes are implemented on a uniform basis. This has resulted in wastage.

(3) Monitoring of the schemes is one of the important components of the programme (which is not in practice in the study area). The monitoring mechanism needs to be strenghtened. The present system of Panchayati Raj can be effectively involved for this purpose.

(4) The study indicates that the role of financial institutions in implementing IRDP seems to be quite satisfactory, particularly in the case of RRBs. These institutions should be involved actively (particularly RRBs with sufficient staff, funds etc.), starting from identification of beneficiaries down to financing and monitoring of the schemes. The field data and the observations reveal that RRBs can shoulder the responsibility of implementing IRDP more cost-effectively/efficiently in rural India.

(5) The schemes on allied agricultural activities are picking up through IRDP and considerable number of beneficiaries have benefited from the programme in general and the poorest of the poor in particular. This trend can be further strengthened through imparting adequate link-

ages like marketing of the products and providing working capital and raw materials required. Absence of supporting services for pursuing non-farm activities has weakened the IRDP.

(6) IRDP beneficiaries should be selected at the Grama Sabha meetings only. The list of beneficiaries should be published, after identification, in the local newspaper or pamphlets and also displayed on the notice board of the village panchayat/mandal office. This helps, to a considerable extent, in reducing the leakage of IRDP funds to the non-poor. Some of the medium and large farmers have deliberately divided their land among the family members (though all living together) on record to avail of IRDP benefits. A mechanism needs to be evolved to eliminate such of those beneficiaries who are non-poor.

(7) In order to prevent disposing of the animals during droughts because of fodder problem, the implementing agency can start *Goshalas* (all the IRDP animals can be pooled to provide fodder at a particular place) and accessability over Common Property Resources (CPRs) in the rural areas. Added to this, care should be taken to provide proper veterinary facilities in villages.

Bibliography

DRD : Department of Rural Development.
EPW : Economic and Political Weekly.
IJAE : Indian Journal of Agricultural Economics.
ISEC : Institute for Social and Economic Change.
ISEI : Inter State Economic Indicators.

Adams, John and Hanumappa, H G (1985) : "Economy and Geography in Karnataka : Spatial Patterns of Development", *Asian Journal of Economics and Social Studies*, Vol.4, No.3, pp.222-248.

Adamsmith, (1776) : *Wealth of Nations*, Everymans Library, New York, referred the new edition 1976.

Adelman, I, et.al. (1985) : "Some Dynamic Aspects of Rural Poverty in India", *EPW*, Vol.XX, No.39, September 28.

Agarwal, A K (1988) : "Rural Poverty and Development : Some Issues", *Southern Economist*, Vol.XXVI, Nos.19 & 20, February 19.

Ahluwalia, M S : (1978) "Rural Poverty and Agricultural Performance in India". *Journal of Development Studies* Vol 14, No 3, pp 298-323.

Ahmed, M and N Bhattacharya (1974) : "Size Distribution of Per Capita Personal Income in India : 1956-57, 1960-61 and 1963-64" *Sankhya : The Indian Journal of Statistics*, Vol.36, Series C. pp. 167-182.

Ahuja, K and P Bhargava (1983) : "Integrated Rural Development Programme : An Evaluation, Jaipur District, *Research Report*,

Institute of Development Studies, Jaipur.

Alagh Y K : "Regional Dimensions of Indian agriculture in Lucas", in Y K Alagh et.al., (ed.) *The Indian Economy : Recent Developments and Future Proposals*, Westview Press, Boulder, 1988.

Alamgir, M (1978) : Bangladesh : A Case of Below Poverty Level Equilibrium Trap, Bangladesh Institute of Development Studies, Dhaka.

Anees, Arui (1988) : "Economic Potential of Dairy Scheme in Alleviating Rural Poverty : Some Methodological Considarations", *Journal of Rural Development*, Vol.8, No.2. pp.167-80.

Anwer, et.al. : "Interaction Between Public Agencies and the Disadvantaged Groups in Markaz Programme in Pakistan", in *UN Poverty Productivity and Participation*, ESCAP, Bangkok, 1982.

Aranha, T J and G K Kaundinya (1985) : "Evaluation of IRDP in Thane District (Maharashtra)", *Research Report*, College of Social Work, Bombay.

Asian Development Bank, *Annual Report : 1988*, ADB Geneva.

————————————, *Annual Report*, Reviewed in Indian Express, 25th April, 1989.

Aynes, Robert L (1989) : *Banking on the Poor*, MIT Press, Cambridge.

Aziz, Abdul, : "Integrated Rural Development Programme" in V M Rao and Abdul Aziz (ed.) *Poverty Alleviation in India : Programmes and Action*, Ashish Publishing House, New Delhi, 1989, pp.102-38.

Aziz, Saej (1978) : *Rural Development: Learning from China*, MacMillan, London.

Bagchee, Sandeep (1987) : "Poverty Alleviation Programmes in Seventh Plan : An Appraisal", *EPW*, Vol.XXII, No.4, January 24.

Balaramulu, C H (1988) : "Evaluation of IRDP in Nalgonda District of Andhra Pradesh : Case Study of a Public Policy" *Research Report*, Centre for Economic and Social Studies, Hydrabad (Mimeo).

Balisher and Roshan Singh (1984) : "Integrated Rural Development Programme Financing by State Bank of India in Bichapur Block of Agra District", *Financing Agriculture*, July-September.

Bandyopadhyay, D (1986) : "Land Reforms in India : An Analysis", *EPW*, Vol.XXI, Nos 25 and 26, January 21-28.

Banerjee, Sumanta (1991) : "Complexities of Organising Rural Poor", *EPW*, Vol.XXVI, No.45, November 9, p.2569.

Bardhan, P K (1970) : "On the Minimum Level of Living and the Rural Poor", *Indian Economic Review*, Vol.5.

——————(1973) :, "On the Incidence of Poverty in Rural India in the Sixties", *EPW*, Annual Number.

—————— (1974) : "Poverty and Income Distribution in India : A Review" in P K Bardhan and T N Srinivasan (ed.), *Poverty and Income Distribution in India*, Statistical Publishing Society, Calcutta.

—————— (1986) : *Land, Labour and Rural Poverty : Essays in Development Economics*, Oxford University Press, Bombay.

Bawer, John et.al. (1992) : Poverty in Philippines : The Impact of Family Size, Asia -Pacific Population and Policy, Population Institute of East-West Center, No.21, Hawai, June.

Bhatty, I Z (1974) : "Some Aspects of Inequalities in Living Standards in Rural India", *Sankhya*, Vol.36, Parts 2 and 4, Part C, p.292.

Bhagwati, J N (1988) : "Poverty and Public Policy", *World Development*, Vol.16, No.5.

Bhanoji Rao, V V, (1981) : Measurmenet of Deprivation and Poverty Based on the Proportion Spent on Food : An Exploratory Exercise", *World Development*, Vol.9, No.4, pp.337-53.

——————, The Forth Coming Book on *Indian Development Framework : Directions for 1990's and Beyond* (Tata McGraw Hill, New Delhi, 1993).

Blarel, et.al. (1992) : "The Economics of Farm Fragmentation : Evidence from Ghana and Rwanda", *The World Bank Economic Review*, Vol.6, No.2, May. pp.233-54.

Boserup, Easter (1970) : _*Women's Role in Economic Development, Reprinted*, George Allen and Unwin, London.

Bowander, B et.al., (1987) : "Further Evidence on the Impact of Dairy Development Programme", *EPW*, (Review of Agriculture), Vol.XXII, No.13, March 28.

Braun, J V et.al. (1992) : "Improving Food Security of the Poor : Concept, Policy, and Programs", International Food Policy Research Institute, Washington. DC, p.9.

Burki, S J (1990) : Development Strategies for Poverty Alleviation, *Asian Development Review*, Vol.8, No.1.

Busink, William C F (1980) : "Reflections on Socio-Economic Development and Poverty in East Asia", in World Bank Staff Working Paper No.406, *Poverty and the Development of Human Resources: Regional Perspectives*, Washington, DC.

Canara Bank (1984) : "Role of Canara Bank in IRDP : An Evaluation in Kolar District", Report prepared by Multi Projects and Development Consultancy Private Limited, Bangalore, November.

————————, (1984) : Impact Study on IRDP in Tirunelveli and Periyar Districts (Tamil Nadu), Bangalore.

Canara Bank Study (1983) : "Impact on IRDP in Tirunalvelli and Periyar Districts", Madras.

Census of India, 1981, quoted in *Inter State Economic Indicators, (ISEI).*

————————, 1981, quoted in *ISEI*, p.8.

Centre for Development Studies (1977) : *Poverty, Unemployment and Development Policy : A Study of Selected Issues with Reference to Kerala*, Orient Longman, Madras.

————————,(1983):Evaluation of IRDP in Quilon District, *Research Report*, Trivandrum.

Chambers, Robert, "Seasonality, Poverty and Nutrition : A Professional Frontier", in S Neelakantan (ed.) *Poverty and Malnutrition*, Tamil Nadu Agricultural University, Coimbatore, 1983.

Chaudhury, R H, "Population Pressure, Agrairan Structure and Productivity", in Gerry Roders (ed.) *Population Growth and poverty in rural South Asia*, Sage Publications, New Delhi, 1989.

Chelliah, Raja J (1960) : *Fiscal Policy in Underdeveloped Countries*, Allen & Unwin Limited, London.

CMIE, *Basic Statistics*, Vol.2, September 1988.

————, *Basic Statistics*, Vol.2, September 1988, quoted in *ISEI*, p.35.

————, *Basic Statistics*, Vol.2, September 1988, p.35.

Dandekar, V M (1982) : "Measurement of Poverty", *EPW*, July 25.

————————, (1982a) : "On Measurement of Undernutritiion", *EPW*, Vol.XVII, No.6, February 6.

————————, (1986) : "Agriculture, Employment, and Poverty", *EPW*, Vol.XXI, Nos.38-39, September 20-27.

Dandekar, V M and N Rath, (1971) : "Poverty in India", *EPW*, January 2 & 9.

————————, (1971a) : *Poverty in India*, Indian School of Political Economy, Poona.

Dantwala, M L (1973) : "Poverty and Unemployment in Rural India", Report Prepared with the Assistance of International Development Research Centre, Ottawa, Canada.

————————, (1973) : *Poverty in India : Then and Now 1870-1970*, MacMillan, New Delhi.

————————, (1983) : "Rural Development : Investment without Organisation" *EPW*, Vol.XVIII, No.18, April 30.

————————, (1985) : "Garibi Hatao Strategy Options", *EPW*, Vol.XX, No.11, March 16-23.

————————, (1987) : "IRDP and Village Structure", *EPW*, May 30.

Das Gupta, R (1981) : "A Cross Sectional Analysis of Poverty and Under-Nutrition in Rural India", Working Paper No.126, Centre for Development Studies, Trivandrum.

Datta, K L (1979) : 'Measurement of Poverty in India : State-wise Estimates", in R K Sinha (ed.) *Economic Development Planning and Policy in India*, Vol.5, *Poverty and Development*, Deep and Deep, New Delhi.

Davis, Deborah and Friedman (1978) : "Welfare Practices in Rural China", *World Development*, Vol.6, No.5.

Dayal, E (1989) : "Rural Poverty in India : A Regional Analysis", *Journal of Rural Studies*, Vol.5, No.1.

Department of Rural Development, (1987) : Ministry of Agriculture, Government of India, *Manual On IRDP and Allied Programmes*, New Delhi, p.2.

————————, (1989) : Ministry of Agriculture, Government of India, *Gramin Vikas News Letter*, Vol.7, No.10, July.

Desai, A R (1987) : "Rural Development and Human Rights", *EPW*, Vol.XXII, No.31.

Deshpande, V N (1981) : "Poverty Studies in India : Issues of Concept and Method", *State and Society*, Vol.2, No.4, October-December.

Desinga Raj (1987) : *Development Programme in Agriculture and the Weaker Sections*, Chungh Publications, Allahabad, pp.6-8.

Dev, S Mahendra, et.al. (1991) : *Rural Poverty in India : Incidence, Issues and Policies*, Discussion paper No.55, Indira Gandhi Institute of Development Research, Bombay, June.

Deverenx, S and H Ray, *The Origins of Famine*, Queen Elizebeth House, Oxford.

Dharmalingam T & P R Dutt, "Interplay of Sanitation, Health and Nutrition" in S Neelakantan (ed.) *Poverty and Malnutrition*, op.cit.

Directorate of Economics and Statistics (1985) : *Bulletin on Food Statistics*, Department of Agriculture and Co-operation, Ministry of Agriculture, Government of India, quoted in *ISEI*, p.36.

Doner, P and W C Thieserhusen, (1990) : "Selected Land Reforms in East and South East Asia : Their Origins and Impact" *Asian Pacific Economic Literature*, Vol.4, No.1, March.

Donoyan, W G (1974) : "Employment Generation in Agriculture : A Study in Mandya District, South India", *Ph D Thesis*, submitted to Cornell University, USA.

Dreze, Jean and Harris Gazadar, (1992) : "Hunger and Poverty in Iraq 1991", *World Development*, Vol.20, No.7, pp.921-45.

Dutt, R C (1973) : *Economic History of India in the Victorian Age*, Vol.II, Seventh (ed.), Routledge and Kegan Paul, 1950, London.

Economic Survey 1990-91, Government of India, New Delhi, 1991, p.69.

Engels, Friedrich (1972, 1984) : *The Origin of the Family, Private Property and the State, Reprinted*, International Publishers, New York, 1972.

Escher, H (1986) : "The Integrated Rural Development Programme in India : Viswa Village Study of Hingaon (Maharastra), Verlag weltarchir, Germen Federal Republic, Stremberg, Quoted in *Rural Development Abstract*, Vol.12, No.1, 1989.

Fields, G S (1980) : *Poverty, Inequality and Development*, Cambridge Univeristy Press, Cambridge.

——————, (1989) : "Changes in Poverty and Inequality in Developing Countries", Cornell University, (Mimeo).

Financial Express, 4.11.1990, for the year 1987-88, this is quoted in *Inter State Economic Indicators* 1990, Planning Department, Government of Karnataka, Bangalore. Government of India, (1974) *Towards Equality : Report of the Committee on the Status of Women in India*, Department of Social Welfare, New Delhi.

——————, 4.4.1990, for the year 1987-88 and quoted in *Interstate Economic Indicators*, Planning Department, Government of Karnataka, 1990, p.6.

Finsterbusch, K and Warren A Van Wieklin II (1989) : "Beneficiary Participation in Development Projects : Emperical Tests of Popular Theories", *Economic Development and Cultural Change*, Vol.37, No.3, April.

Frank, A G (1976) : *On Capitalistic Under Development*, Oxford University Press, Bombay.

Fuchs, Victor R (1967) : "Redefining Poverty and Redistributing Income", *The Public Interest*, National Bureau of Economic Research, Quoted in Will and Vatter (ed.) *Poverty in Affluence*,

Harcenk, Brau and World Inc., New York.

Gadam, S (1986) : "Evaluation Study of Integrated Rural Development Programme (Sangli District)", Gokhale Institute of Politics and Economics, Pune, August (Mimeograph Series No.24).

George, H (1879, 1981) : *Progress and Poverty*, Robert Schalkenbach Foundation, New York.

Gianchandani, D et.al. (1987) : "A Target Missed : An Evaluation of IRDP in Northern and Eastern Rajasthan" *Research Report*, Institute of Development Studies, Jaipur, September.

Gopalam, Coluther and Kamala S Jaya Rao (1984) : "Classification of Undernutrition, their Limitation and Fallacies", *Journal of Tropical Padiatrics*, Vol.XXX, February.

Gouri, R D (1988) : *Extent and Measurement of Poverty in India*, Mittal Publications, New Delhi.

Government of India, Agricultural Labour Enquiry, 1950-51.

—————, (1954) : *All India Rural Credit Survey : Report of the Committee of the Director*, A D Gorwala, Bombay, Reserve Bank of India India, Bombay.

—————, (1961) : "Report of the Study Group on the Welfare of the Weaker Sections of the Village Community", Ministry of Community Development and Co-operation, New Delhi.

—————, (1977) : *All-India Debt and Investment Survey 1971-72*, RBI, Bombay.

—————, (1978) : *Regional Rural Banks : Report of the Review Committee*, (Chairman M L Dantwala) RBI, Bombay.

—————, (1981) : *Report of the Committee to Review Arrangements for Institutional Credut for Agriculture and Rural Development (CRAFICARD)*, RBI, Bombay, Chairman B Sivaraman, January.

—————, (1982) : *Report of the Expert Group on Programme for Alleviation of Poverty*, Planning Commission, New Delhi, February.

—————, (1985) : "Evaluation Report on Integrated Rural Development Programme", Programme Evaluation Organisation, Planning Commission, New Delhi, May.

—————, (1985) : *Report of the Committee to Reviw the Existing Administrative Arrangements for Rural Development and Poverty Alleviation Programmes*, (CAAD)", DRD, Ministry of Agriculture, New Delhi, December.

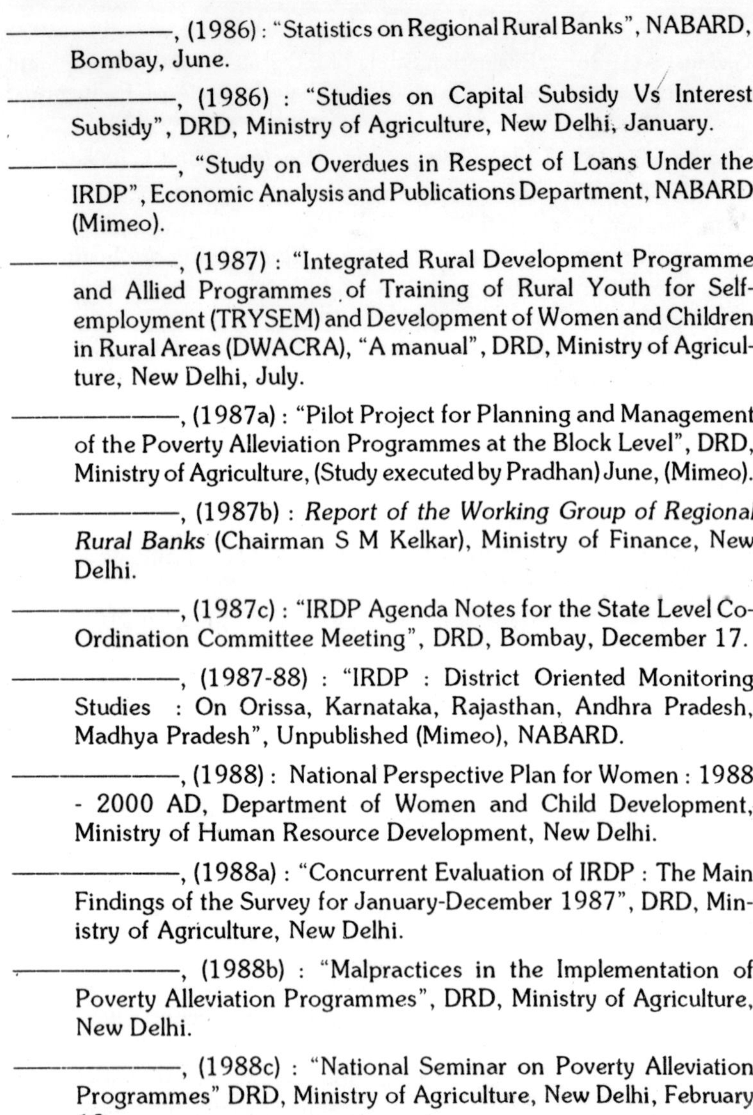

———————, (1986) : "Statistics on Regional Rural Banks", NABARD, Bombay, June.

———————, (1986) : "Studies on Capital Subsidy Vs Interest Subsidy", DRD, Ministry of Agriculture, New Delhi, January.

———————, "Study on Overdues in Respect of Loans Under the IRDP", Economic Analysis and Publications Department, NABARD (Mimeo).

———————, (1987) : "Integrated Rural Development Programme and Allied Programmes of Training of Rural Youth for Self-employment (TRYSEM) and Development of Women and Children in Rural Areas (DWACRA), "A manual", DRD, Ministry of Agriculture, New Delhi, July.

———————, (1987a) : "Pilot Project for Planning and Management of the Poverty Alleviation Programmes at the Block Level", DRD, Ministry of Agriculture, (Study executed by Pradhan) June, (Mimeo).

———————, (1987b) : *Report of the Working Group of Regional Rural Banks* (Chairman S M Kelkar), Ministry of Finance, New Delhi.

———————, (1987c) : "IRDP Agenda Notes for the State Level Co-Ordination Committee Meeting", DRD, Bombay, December 17.

———————, (1987-88) : "IRDP : District Oriented Monitoring Studies : On Orissa, Karnataka, Rajasthan, Andhra Pradesh, Madhya Pradesh", Unpublished (Mimeo), NABARD.

———————, (1988) : National Perspective Plan for Women : 1988 - 2000 AD, Department of Women and Child Development, Ministry of Human Resource Development, New Delhi.

———————, (1988a) : "Concurrent Evaluation of IRDP : The Main Findings of the Survey for January-December 1987", DRD, Ministry of Agriculture, New Delhi.

———————, (1988b) : "Malpractices in the Implementation of Poverty Alleviation Programmes", DRD, Ministry of Agriculture, New Delhi.

———————, (1988c) : "National Seminar on Poverty Alleviation Programmes" DRD, Ministry of Agriculture, New Delhi, February 12.

Government of Karnataka (1988) : *Perspective Plan 2001*, Report of the Expert Group, Government of Karnataka, Bangalore, October, Table-3, p.22c.

Government of Uttar Pradesh (1987) : "Summary and Conclusions and Recommendations on IRDP Based on Evaluation Studies", State

Institute of Rural Development, Lucknow.

Griffen, Keith (1988) : "Development Strategies Choosing the Right One", *The Economic Times*, August 4.

Guhan, S (1987) : "Aid for the Poor : Performance and Possibilities in India", Madras Institute of Development Studies, Madras, December (Mimeo).

Gumaste, V M et.al. (1987) : *Intervention and Poverty*, IFMR Publications, Madras.

——————, *Annual Report 1985-86* of Department of Rural Development, Ministry of Agriculture, New Delhi.

Hadimani, R N, S Erappa and N K M Yadav (1985) : "Sericulture as a Leverage of Social Mobility Among Scheduled Castes in Rural Areas", *Journal of Institute of Economic Research*, No.20, 1 & 2.

Hadimani R N (1983) : Poverty and Backwardness Among Ganigas in Karnataka", *The Mysore Economic Review*, Vol.68, No.10, October.

——————, (1984) : *The Politics of Poverty*, Ashish Publishing House, New Delhi.

Hanumantha Rayappa, P and R Muthurayappa (1986) : *Backwardness and Welfare of Scheduled Castes and Scheduled tribes in India*, Ashish Publishing House, New Delhi.

Hanumappa, H G (1978) : "Income Distribution in Urban Areas : A Case Study of Bangalore", *EPW*, Vol.XIII, No.15, April 15, pp.662-66.

——————, (1979) : "Rural Credit System and The Rural Poor", *Behavioural Sciences and Rural Development*, Vol.2, No.2, pp.116-24.

——————, "The Impact of Small Farmers Development Agency (SFDA) Programmes on the Rural Poor", in S Neelakantan (ed.) *Poverty and Malnutrition*, Tamil Nadu Agricultural University, Coimbatore, pp.197-207.

——————, (1982) "Inter-village Differences in Development", Paper prsented at *National Seminar on Political Economy of Development*, University of Hyderabad, Hydrabad, January 7-9.

Hanumappa, H G and K N Ninan (1982) : "Rural Poor and Institutional Credit : Where do we go from here?", *The Asian Journal of Economics*, Vol.I, No.3, September.

——————, (1984) : "Socio-Economic Dimensions of Rural Housing in Karnataka", *Unpublished Research Report*, ISEC, Bangalore.

Hanumappa, H G and J Adams, (1980) : "Two Karnataka Villages and the Outside World", paper presented at International Symposium, *The External Dimension in Rural South Asia*, University of London, London, December 11-13.

Haq, M (1976) : *Poverty Curtain : Choices for the Third World*, Columbia University Press, New York.

Haque, T and G Parthasarathy (1992) : "Land Reform and Rural Development Highlights of a National Seminar", *EPW*, Vol.27, No.8, February 22.

Harrington, M (1968) :, *Citizens Board of Inquiry Into Hunger and Malnutrition in the United States*, New Community Press, Washington.

Hayami, Y and V W Ruttan, (1971) : *Agricultural Development : An International Perspective*, The John Hopkins Press, Baltimore.

Hayami, Yujiro and Masao Kikuchi (1981) :, *Asian Village Economy at the Cross Roads : An Economic approach to Institutional Change*, University of Tokyo Press, Tokyo.

Hemalatha Rao (1981) : *Regional Disparties and Development in India*, Ashish Publishing House, New Delhi, pp. 302-316.

Higgins, B (1958) : *Economic Development : Principles, Problems and Policies*, Third Indian Reprint, Central Book Depot, Allahabad, 1966.

Hirway, Indira (1983) : "Programmes for Poverty Erradication : A Critique of Target Group Approach", *Research report*, Sardar Patel Institute of Economic and Social Research, Ahmedabad (Mimeo)

————————,(1984) : "Group Approach : A Study in Gujarat", *IJAE*, July-September.

————————, (1984) :" Special Employment Programmes in Rural Development : A Study of NREP in Gujarat", *Unpublished Research Report*, Sardar Patel Institute of Economic and Social Research, Ahmedabad.

————————,(1985) : Garibi Hatao : Strategy of IRDP", *EPW*, Vol.XX, No.11.

————————, (1985) : "Garibi Hatao : Can IRDP Do It?" *EPW*, Vol.XX, NO.11, March 30.

————————(1986) : *Abolition of Poverty in India*, Vikas Publishing, New Delhi.

————————(1988) : "Reshaping IRDP : Some Issues", *EPW*, June 25.

Hossain, Mahabub (1988) : "Credit for Alleviation of Rural Poverty : The Grameen Bank in Bangladesh", *Research Report 65*, International Food Policy Research Institute, Washington DC, February.

Husaini, Ishrat (1992) : "Adjustment and the Impact on the Poor : The Case of Africa", A Paper presented at African Development Bank, Abidjan, March 9-12. p.11.

International Labour Organisation (1977) : Poverty and Landlessness in Rural Asia, Geneva.

————————,(1979) : Profiles of Rural Poverty, Geneva.

————————, (1986) : *Fighting Poverty : Asia's major Challenge*, ARTEP, New York.

Institute of Financial Management and Research (1984) : "An Economic Assessment of Poverty Eradication and Rural Unemployment Alleviation Programmes and Their Prospects", Madras, April.

Institutional Finance and Statistics Department, (1985) : "Evaluation of Integrated Rural Development Programme" Government of Karnataka, Bangalore.

Iyengar, N S and M Mukherjee (1961) : "A note on the deprivation of size distribution of Personal Household Income from a given size distribution of consumer expenditure", paper presented at the Second Econometric Conference, Waltair.

Jain, L C (1988) : "Poverty, Environment Development : A View from Gandhi's Window", *EPW*, February 13.

Jain, S C (1983) : Impact Study of Integrated Rural Development Programme, Uchchhal Taluk, Surat, Gujarat, South Gujarat University, (Mimeo).

Jain, S K (1985) : "Banking Facilities for the Weaker Sections of Society : A Study of DRI Scheme", *Unpublished Research Report*, ISEC, Bangalore.

Jodha, N S (1986) : "Common Property Resources and Rural Poor in Dry Regions of India", *EPW*, July 5.

Jorgenson, D W (1961) : "The Development of a Dual Economy", *Economic Journal*, Vol.71, June.

Kale, B D and J B Hosalkar (1976) : "Employment and Wage Among Rural Labourers", *Unpublished Research Report*, JSS Institute of Economic Research, Dharwad, Karnataka.

Kakwani, N and K Subba Rao, (1990) : "Rural Poverty and Its Alleviation in India", *EPW*, Vol.XXV, No.3, March 31, A 2-16.

————————, (1992) : "Rural Poverty and Its Alleviation in India", *EPW*, Vol.XXVII, No.18, May 2, pp.971-2.

Karnataka State Janata Party (1987) : "Loan Melas for Whose Benefit?" (Collection of Newspaper articles), February.

Karnataka State Gazetteer Part I (1982) : Karnataka Gazetteer Department, Government of Karnataka, Bangalore, **Chief Editor, S V** Kamath.

Kerala Planning Board Survey (1981) : Integrated Rural Development Programme : Kerala, Evaluation Division, Government of Kerala, Trivandrum.

Keynes, J M (1973) : *The General Theory of Employment Interest and Money*, MacMillan, London.

Khan, A R, Growth and Inequaltiy in the Rural Philippines", ILO Study on *Poverty and Landlessness in Rural Asia*, Geneva, 1977.

Khan, A R (1979) : "The Comilla Model and the Integrated Rural Development Programme of Banglaesh : An Experiment in Co-operative Capitalism", *World Development*, Vol.17, April-May.

Khan, A R and Eddy Lee (ed.) (1984) : *Poverty in Asia*, International Labour Oganisation, Bangkok.

Khan, O M (1985) : "A Model of Endowment - Constrained Demand for Food in an Agricultural Economy with Empirical Applications to Bangladesh", *World Development*, No.13.

Kothari, Rajani (1988) : *State Against Democracy*, Ajantha Publications, New Delhi.

Kravis, Irving B (1960) : "International Differences in the Distribution of Income", *Review of Economics and Statistics*, Vol.XLII, No.4, November.

Krishna Raj (1976) : "Growth Investment and Poverty in Sixth Plan", *EPW*, Vol.XVIII, No.47.

Krishnan, A C Kutty (1984) : "A Case Study of Integrated Rural Development Programme in a Kerala Village", *IJAE*, October-December.

Krueger, Anue O (1990) : "Government Failures in Development", *A Journal of American Economic Association*, Vol.4, No.3, Summer p.3-9.

Kulkarni P M (ND) : "A Scheme for Allevation of Extreme Poverty : An Evaluation", *Unpublished Research Report*, Institute for Social and Economic Change, Bangalore.

————————(1988) : "Bonded Labourers : Release and Rehabilitation" in V M Rao and Abdul Aziz (ed.) *Poverty Alleviation in India : Programmes and Action*, Ashish Publishing House, New Delhi, 1989.

Kumar, B (1987) : "Evaluation of Poverty Alleviation Programmes in Faizabad Commissionery", *Research Report*, Govind Ballabh Pant Social Science Institute, Allhabad (Mimeo).

Kumar, B G (1986) : "Ethiopian Famines 1973-85 : A Case Study", *WIDER* Conference Paper.

Kurian, C T (1978) : *Poverty Planning and Social Transformation*, Allied Publishers, New Delhi.

Kurian, N J (1987) :, "IRDP : How Relevant Is It?", EPW, Vol.XXII, No.52, December 26, A-161 - A-176. (p. A-170).

Kuznets, Simon (1974) : "Demographic Aspects of Size Distribution of Income : An Exploratory Essay", *Economic Development and Cultural Change*, Vol.25, No.1, October. Quoted by H G Hanumappa (1978) "Income Distribution in Urban Areas : A Case Study of Bangalore", *op.cit.*

Lal, Deepak (1984) : "Trends in Real Wages in Rural India 1980-1980", Development Research Department Discussion Paper No. 103, World bank, Washington DC.

Laxminarayana, H (1973) :, "Small Farmers Development Programme", *EPW*, April 28, p.806.

Lea, David A M and D P Chaudhuri (1983) : *Rural Development and the State : Contraditions and Dilemmas in Developing Countries*, Methuen, London, p.19 and 24.

Lewis, W A (1954) : "Economic Development with Unlimited Supplies of Labour", *The Manchester School of Economics and Social Studies*, Vol 22, May, pp 139-191.

Lewis, Oscar (1969) : "The Culture of Poverty", in Daniel P Moynihan (ed) *On Understanding Poverty, Basic Books*, New York, pp.187-200.

Lipton, Michael (1978) : *Why Poor People Stay Poor, A Study of Urban Bias in World Development*, Temple Smith, London.

Lokanathan, P S (1967) : "Pattern of Income Distribution and Saving", Occassional Paper 21, NCAER (Sir Williams Meyer Endowment Lectures, 1966-67).

Lynn Bennett (1992) : "Women, Poverty and Productivity in India", An EDI Seminar Paper No.43, Economic Development Institute, The World Bank, Washington, DC.

Maheswari, S R (1985) : *Rural Development in India : A Public Policy Approach*, Sage Publications, New Delhi, p.40.

Maithani, B P and K Haloi (1988) : "Implementation of IRDP : Nagaland Experience", *Journal of Rural Development*, vol.7, No.6.

Malhotra, R N (1986) : "The role of Banking in Rural Development", *RBI Bulletin*, September.

Malyadri, P (1988) : "Financing Pig Farming : A Study", *Kurukshethra*, Vol. XXXVII, No.3, December.

Malthus, T R (1820, 1914) : *An Essay on the Principle of Population*, In Two Volumes, Volume Two, Everyman's Liberary, London, p.48.

Mathur, P N (1984) : "Economics of Social Forestry with Special Reference to Meghalaya", paper presented at The National Seminar on development Strategies for the North-East Regional NEHU Shillong, Jointly Organised by the Indian Economic Association and Planning Commission, Government of India, April.

Marshall, Alfred (1891, 1977) : *Principles of Economics* (Eighth Edition), MacMillan Press Limited, London.

Martin Rein, "Problems in Definition on Measurements of Poverty", in Peter Townsend (ed) : *The Concept of Poverty*, op.cit.

Matson, Jim and Mark Selden (1992) : "Poverty and Inequality in China and India", *EPW*, Vol.XXVII, No.14, April 4, pp.701-15.

Meier, Gerald M (1964, 1984) : *Leading Issues in Economic Development*, Oxford University Press, Inc, New York.

Meliczek, Hans (1984) : "Guidelines for the Evaluation of Agrarian Reforms and Rural Development", *Development and Cooperation*, No.6, November/December, Quoted in CIRDAP, *News Letter*, July 21, 1985, p.15 & 18.

Miller, S M et.al. " A Social Indicators Defintion" in Wills and Vatter (ed.), *Poverty in Affluence*, Hareatt Brave and World, Inc., New York.

Mellor, J W (1988) : "The Inter-Twining of Environmental Problems and Poverty", *Environment*, November.

Minhas, B S (1974) : *Planning and the Poor*, Sultan Chand, New Delhi.

————————, (1974a) : "Rural Poverty, Land Distribution and Development Strategies : Facts", *Sankhya*, Vol.36, Series C, Parts 2 & 4.

Minhas, B S, L R Jain, S D Tendulkar (1991) : "Declining Incidence of Poverty in 1980's : Evidence Versus Artefacts", *EPW*, Vol.XXVI, Nos.27 and 28, July 6-13, pp.1673-82.

Ministry of Agriculture, Government of India (1989) : *Report of the Working Group on Land Reforms for the Eighth Five Year Plan 1990-95)*, New Delhi, p.1.

Mohanlal, G M (1988) : *Poverty Alleviation : The Indian Experience*,

Himalaya Publishing House, Delhi.

Mohan Das, M (1988) : "Rural Poverty, Some Conceptual Issues", paper presented in the National Seminar on *Rural Poverty and Area Planning*, at Post-graduate Dept. of Economics, Machilipatnam, Jan 14-16.

Mukherjee, B (1967) : *Community Development in India*, Orient Longman, Calcutta, pp. 1-2.

Mukherjee, M (1969) : *National Income of India, Trends and Structure*, Statistical Publishing Co., Calcutta.

Myrdal, G (1970) : *The Challenge of World Poverty*, Panthean Books, New York.

—————————,(1973) : *Against to Stream ; Critical Essays on Economics*, Macmillan.

—————————, (1985) : *Asian Drama*, Vol VII, Kalyani Publishers, New Delhi.

Natonal Bank for Agriculture and Rural Development, (NABARD) (1984) "Study of Implementation of Integrated Rural Development Programme", (Mimeo), NABARD, Bombay, p.11.

—————————, (1988) : National Bank News Review, Vo.4, No.7, September.

Nagarajan, V (1983), "National Food Security System" in S Neelakantan (ed.), op.cit.

Naidu, I J (1975) : All-India Report on agricultural Census, 1970-71, Ministry of Agriculture and Irrigation, Department of Irrigation, Government of India, New Delhi.

Naik, Vijay and Shailaja Prasad (1984) : "On Levels of Living of Scheduled Castes and Scheduled Tribes", *EPW*, Vol.90, No.30.

Narayan, K V et.al. (1989) : "Development Schemes for Rural Poor : A Study", *Kurukshetra*, April.

National Institute of Rural Development, (1984) : "Employment and Income Generation Under IRDP and NREP/DRI : A Study in Karnataka", Hydarabad.

National Sample Survey Data 11th Round 1956-57, Report No.140, Vaidyanathan used the above report and also NSS data of 14th round and drawn similar findings regarding the percentage of the poor. For details see Vaidyanathan A.

Nayak, P J and Sumithra (1985) : *Constructing the Poverty Line : A New Approach with Application to Karnataka*, Planning Department, Government of Karnataka, Bangalore.

Neelakantan, S (ed.) (1983) : *Poverty and Malnutrition*, Tamil Nadu Agricutlrual University, Coimbatore.

Nurkse R (1953) : *Problems of Capital Formation in Underdeveloped Countries*, Basil Blackwell, Oxford.

Ojha, P D (1986) : "Agricultural Credit Institutions : India (Their Structure and Role in Development", *Reserve Bank of India Bulletin*, February, p.150-74.

Orshansky, M (1975) : "Counting the Poor : Another Look at the Poverty Profile", *Social Security Bulletin*, Quoted in A B Atkinsen (ed.), *The Economics of Inequality*, Oxford University Press.

——————, (1968) : "The Shape of Poverty in 1966", *Social Security Bulletin*, March, p.4.

Oshima, Harry T (1962) : "The International Comparision of Size Distribution of Family Incomes with Special Reference to Asia", *Review of Economics and Statistics*, Vol.XLIV, No.4, November.

Oughton, L (1982) : "The Maharastra Droughts of 1970-73 : An Analaysis of Scarcity", *Oxford Bulletin of Economics and Statistics*, No.44.

Otto Blume, "The Poverty of Old People in Urban and Rural Areas" in Peter Townsend (ed.) op.cit.

Paniker, P G K (1980) : "Inter Regional Variations in Calorie Intake", Working Paper No.3, Centre for Development studies, Trivandrum.

Parthasarathy, G (1976) : "Land Reform and the Changing Agrairan Structure", in Shah, C H and C N Vakil (ed.) *Agricultural Development of India : Policy and Problems*, Reprinted in Uma Kapila (ed.) *Indian Economy Since Independence*, Acadamic Foundation, Delhi, 1990.

——————, (1991) : "Lease Market, Poverty Alleviation and Policy Options", *EPW*, Vol.XXVI, No.13, March 30.

——————, (1992) : "Roots of Naxalism", *Frontline*, February 14.

——————, "Integrated Rural Development Concept, Theoretical Base and Contribution" in D B Gupta et.al. (ed.) *Development Planning and Policy : Essays in Honour of Professor V K R V Rao*, Wiley Eastern Limited, New Delhi, 1982.

Parthasarathy, G and D S Prasad (1974) : Response to and Impact of HYV Rice by Size and Tenure in a Delta Village, Andhra Pradesh, India", *Developing Economics*, June.

Parthasarathy, V S (1990) : "Rural Poverty", *Unpublished Research Report*, ISEC, Bangalore, November.

Pathak, B S (1987) : "Rural Development-Need for pragmatic planning", Financial Express, October 2, p.6.

Paukert, Felix (1973) : "Income Distribution at Different Levels of Development : A Survey of the Evidence", *International Labour Review*, Vol.C VIII, No. 2 & 3, August/September.

Paul S (1984) : "Mid-Term Appraisal of the Sixth Plan : Why Poverty Alleviation Lags Behind", *EPW*, Vol.XIX, No.18, May 5.

Payne, Richard J (1980) : "African Economic Problems and the African Position on the Land of the Sea in Relation to Managements Nodules", *The Journal of Developing Areas*, October 15.

Planning Commission (1979) : *Report of the Task Force on Minimum Needs and Effective Consumption Demand*, Government of India, New Delhi.

————————, (1985) : "Evaluation Report of IRDP", Planning and Evaluation Organisation, New Delhi.

————————, (1989) : *Indian Planning Experience - A Statistical Profile*, New Delhi, February. Table 14.1, p.67.

————————, Sixth Five Year Plan, Government of India, p.215.

————————, *Seventh Five Year Plan*, Government of Karnataka, New Delhi, quoted in P H Rayappa and G Nagaraj (1990) *Poverty Alleviation Programmes in India : An Inventory for the Southern States of Karnataka, Kerala, Tamil Nadu and Union Territory of Pondicherry*, prepared for the study group on Anti-Poverty Programmes set-up by the National Commission on Rural Labour, Government India, New Delhi.

Planning Department (1984) : *An Approach to Karnataka's Seventh Five Year Plan 1985-1990*, The Economic and Planning Council, Government of Karnataka, Bangalore, June, p.5.

————————, (1989) : *Inter State Economic Indicators*, Plan Finance and Resources Division, Government of Karnataka, May, Table 1.5, p.8.

————————, *Economic Survey 1991-92*, Government of Karnataka, Bangalore, p.12.

Programme Evaluation Organisation (1985) : "Evaluation Report on IRDP", Planning Commission, New Delhi.

Prebisch, Raul (1959) : "Commercial Policies in the Underdeveloped Countries", *The American Economic Review*, (papers proceedings of the Seventy First Annual Meeting of the *American Economic Association*, Vol.XLIX, No.2, May, pp.251-73.

——————, (1971) : *Change and Development Latin Americas Great Task*, Praeger Publishers, New York, pp.191-213.

Pulley, Robert V (1989) : Making the Poor Credit Worthy : A Case Study of the Integrated Rural Development Program in India, 58 World Banks Discussion Papers, The World Bank, Washington, DC. (p.17).

Radhakrishna, R et.al. (1987) : "Inter-Regional Variations in Welfare Levels and their Contributory Factors", Conference Paper, Andhra Pradesh Economic Association, Vol.II, & V, January 17-18.

Radhakrishna, R and A Sarma (1976) : "Inflation and Disparities in Level of Living, *Indian Economic Journal*, April-July.

Rajasekaran, N, Marshall's Views on Poverty : Its Relevance to India Today", (Forthcoming in *Asian Journal of Economics and Social Studies.*

Ram Reddy, G and G Haragopl (1984) : *Public Policy and Rural Poor in India*, Concept Publication and Centre for Economic and Social Studies, Hydrabad.

Ranade, Sudhamshu (1991) : "Rural Poverty and Its Alleviation in India", *EPW*, Vol.XXVI, No.41, October 12, p.2380.

Ranadive, R R (1972) : "Distribution of Income : Trends Since Planning", (Mimeo), Quoted in Sastry, SAR (1980) "Literature on Poverty Income and Development", *Artha Vijnana*, Vol.22, No.1, March.

Rangaswamy, P (1989) : "Evaluation of IRDP in Haryana", *Research Report*, Agricultural Economics and Research Centre, University of Delhi, Delhi.

Ranis, Gusta V and John C H Fei (1961) :, "A Theory of Economic Development", *American Economic Review* Vol 51, September, pp 533-65.

Rao, C H Hanumantha (1988) : "Current Agrarian Scene : Policy Alternatives", *EPW*, March 26.

——————, (1992) : "Integrating Poverty Alleviation Programmes with Development Strategies Indian Experience", *EPW*, Vol.XXVII, No.4, November 28, pp.2603-7.

Rao, V K R V (1938) : *An Essay on India's National Income*, George Allen and Unwin Ltd.

——————, (1982) : *Food, Nutrition and Poverty in India*, Vikas Publishing House, New Delhi.

Rao V M (1988) : "Interventions for the Poor : Critical Dimensions, Potentialities and Limitations", *EPW*. (Special Number) :.

Rao, V M and Abdul Aziz (ed.) (1987) : *Poverty Alleviation in India Programmes and Action*, Ashish Publishing House, New Delhi.

Rao, V M and S Erappa (1987) : "IRDP and Rural Diversification : A Study in Karnataka", *EPW*, (Review of Agriculture), Vol.XXII, No.52, December 26, A.151-60.

————, (1990) : "Development Opportunities in Dry Land Agriculture", in *Agriculture Development Policies : Adjustments and Reorientation*, The Golden Jublees of the Indian Society of Agriculture Economics, Oxford and IBH Publishing Co.Pvt. Ltd., New Delhi.

Rao, Hanumatha C H and P Rangaswamy (1988) : "Efficiency of Investments in IRDP : A Study of Uttar Pradesh", *EPW*, Vol.1, 2, 3 No.26, A-69 - A-76. (p. A-69).

Rath, Neelakantha (1985) : "Garibi Hatao : Can IRDP Do It? *EPW*, Vol.XX, No.6, February 9.

Ravallion, M (1987) : *Markets and Fanimes*, Clarendon Press, Oxford.

Reddy, M Gopinath (1989) : "Poverty Alleviation Programme in Andhra Pradesh with Special Reference to IRDP : Some Administrative and Institutional Issues", Seminar Paper on Eighth Plan Perspectives of Andhra Pradesh Organised at Centre for Economics and Social Studies, Hydrabad, February 2-3.

Reddy, Ratna V (1988) : "Surplus Labour, Poverty and Agricultural Development", *Artha Vijnana*, Vol.XXX, No.4, December.

Registrar General of India, Quoted in *ISEI*, Planning Department, Government of Karnataka, May 1989, p.16.

Report of Karnataka Third Backward Classes Commission Vol. I, Government of Karnataka, 1990. (Under the Chairmanship of Channappa Reddy).

Report of Karnataka First Backward Classes Commission, Vol.IV, "Socio-Economic Survey Data", Government of Karnataka, Bangalore, 1978.

Report of The Commission of Scheduled Caste and Scheduled Tribes - Eighth Report 1985-86, quoted in *ISEI*, p.115.

Reserve Bank of India (1969) : *Report of the All India Rural Credit Review Committee*, RBI, Bombay, Chaimrman BVenkatappaiah.

————, (1977) : All India Debt and Investment Survey (1971-72), Indebtedness of Rural Households as on June 30, 1971 and Availability of Institutional Finance, Bombay.

————, (1977a) : "Pattern of Assets of Rural Households 1961-71", RBI Staff Occassional Paper, Vol.2, June.

———————, (1978) : *Regional Rural Banks : Report of the Review Committee*, RBI, Bombay.

———————, (1981) : *Report of the Committee to Review Arrangements for Institutional Credit for Agriculture and Rural Development (CRAFICARD)*, RBI, Bombay, January, Chairman B Sivaraman.

Rimlinger, G V (1976) : Smith and their Evils of the Poor, *Review of Social Economy* Vol 34, No 3, December, pp 333-44.

Rosenmayr, Leopold "Cultural Poverty of Working Class Youth", in Peter Townsend (ed.) *The Concept of Poverty*. op.cit.

Rowntree, B S (1941) : *Poverty and Progress*, A Second Social Survey of York, London. p.102-3.

Roy Choudhury, Uma Datta (1977) : "Income Distribution and Economic Development in India since 1950-51", *Indian Economic Journal*, Vol2., No.2, Part II, October-December, p.143.

Sahola, G S (1978) : "Theories of Personal Income Distribution : A Survey", *The Journal of Economic Literature*, Vol.XVI, No.1, March, p.1-55.

Saith, A (1981) : Production, Prices and Poverty in Rural India, *Journal of Development Studies*, Vol 17, No 2, pp 196-213.

Saith, Aswini (1983) : "Development and Distribution : A Critic of the Cross-Country U - Hypothesis", *Journal of Development Economics*, Vol.XIII, pp.367-82.

Sanwal, Mukul (1985) : "Garibi Hatao : Improving Implementation", *EPW*, VolXX, No.49, December 7.

Sarma I R K (1970) : "Composition and Distribution of Personal Income in India", *Unpublished Ph D Thesis*, Delhi University, Delhi.

Satyapriya V S and S Erappa "Land Reforms in India : Some Field Evidence", in A R Raja Purohit, (ed.) : *Land Reforms in India*, Ashish Publishig House, New Delhi, 1984. p.177.

Satyapriya, V S (1979) : *Dimensions of Agricultural Labour in Karnataka*, Sterling Publishers, New Delhi.

Saxena, A P (1987) : "Concurrent Evaluation of IRDP Selected Aspects for Administrative Follow-up", *EPW*, Vol.XXII, No.39, September 21.

Schillor, Broadley, R (1976) : *The Economics of Poverty and Discrimination*, Prentice Hall, New Jersey.

Scott, H (1984) : *Working Your Way to the Bottom : The Feminisation of Poverty*, Pondara Press, London.

Seers, Dudley (1972) : "What are We Trying to Measure? *Reprint 106*, Institute of Development Studies, Sussex.

Sen, A K (1980) : "Levels of Poverty - Policy and Change", World Bank Staff Working Paper, No.401.

——————, (1981) : *Poverty and Famines : An Essay on Entitlements and Deprivation*, Oxford Clerendon Press, Oxford.

——————, (1987) : "Research for Action : Hunger and Entitlement", *World Institute of Development Economic Research (WIDER)*, United Nation University.

Sen, D and P K Das (1988) : "Poverty Alleviation Through Group Farm Forestry : A Case Study", *Journal of Rural Development*, Vol.7, No.6.

Sen Gupata, S and P D Joshi, "Concept of Poverty and Estimates of Poverty at the Regional Levels", in R K Sinha (ed.) (1989), op.cit.

Shah, A M (1973) : *The Household Dimension of the Family in India : A First Study in a Gujarat Village and a Review of Other Studies*, Orient Longman Limited, New Delhi, p.110.

Singer, Hans W (1977) : Poverty, Income Distribution and Levels of Living : Twenty Five Years of Changes in about Development", *The Seoul National University Economic Review*, Vol.XI, No.1, December.

Singh, Kartar (1985) : "Rural Poverty", *The Economic Times*, May, 24-25.

Sinha, R K (1989) : *Economic Development Planning and Policy in India*, Vol. 5, *Poverty and Development* Deep and Deep, New Delhi.

Sivasankaraiah, M and P Ramappa (1989) : "Private Poultry Farms Vs Poultry Farms under IRDP", *Kurukshetra*, Vol.XXXVII, No.4, January.

Smolensky, E (1966) : "Investment in the Education of the Poor : A Pessimistic Report", *American Economic Review*, Supplement LV, May.

Snewden, P (1985) : "The Political Economy of Ethiopian Famine", *National Westminister Bank Quarterly Review* November.

Srinivasan, T N (1983a) : "Measuring Malnutrition", *Ceres*, Vol.XVI, No.2, March-April.

Srinivasan, T N and P K Bardhan (ed.) : (1974) : *Poverty and Income distribution in India*, Statistical Publishing Society, Calcutta.

Srinivsan, K "Rural Development : The Indian Experiments" in K Prasad and S I Patnaik (ed.) : *Rural Development Stragegies for Weaker*

Sections, Dept. of Analytical and Applied Economics, Utkal Univesity, Bhubaneswar 1984.

Sodhi, J S (1988) : "Experiences of the Integrated Rural Development Programme : Some Policy Implications", *Productivity*, Vol.29, No.3, October-December.

———— (1987) : "Evaluation of IRDP in Satara District : Maharastra", *Research Report,* Sri Ram Centre for Industrial relations and Human Resources, New Delhi.

State Bank of Hyderabad (1983) : "Monitoring-Cum-Mid-term Evaluation of IRDP", Hyderabad.

State Bank of India (1987) : "IRDP : An Impact Evaluation Study", *SBI Monthly Review*, August.

Streeten, Paul (1978) : "Editors' Introductions", *World Development*, Vol.6, No.3, pp.241-3.

Subba Rao K (1985) : "Regional Variations in Impact of Programmes : A Review of Evidence", *EPW*, volXX, No.43, October 26.

Sukhatme, P V (1965) : *Feeding India's Growing Millions,* Asia, Bombay.

————, (1978) : "Assessment of Adequacy of Diets at Different Income Levels", *EPW.*

————, (1982) : "Measurement of Undernutrition", *EPW*, Vol.XVIII, No.50, December 22.

Suryanarayana, M H (ND) : "Living Level of Poor in Karnataka", *Unpublished Research Report*, Indian Statistical Institute, Bangalore.

Saminathan, M C "Nutrition Programmes - Experiences in India", in S Neelakantan (ed.) : *Poverty and Malnutrition*, op.cit.

Swamy, Subramanya (1969) : Structural Changes and the Distribution of Income by Size : The Case of India", *Review of Income and Wealth*, Series 13.

Taylor, C et.al. (1965) : *India's Roots of Democracy : A Sociological Analysis of Rural India's Experience in Planned Development Since Independence,* Orient Longman, Calcutta, p.609.

Tendler, Judith (1987) : "What Ever Happened to Poverty Alleviation? Ford Foundation, March, Annex I. p.5.

Tendulkar, Suresh D and L R Jain (1991) : "Change in Number of Rural and Urban Poor Between 1970-71 and 1983" *EPW*, Vol.XXVI, Nos.11 & 12, March, pp.709-22.

Thaha, M "Poverty Alleviation and IRDP in Policy Analysis and Management for Agriculture and Rural Development" (Reading Material for IAS Officers), NIRD, Hyderabad, pp.206-207 (Mimeo).

The Central Bank of India (1983) : "Integrated Rural Development Programme in chindwara District of Madhya Pradesh", Economic Intelligence Department, Bombay.

Thimmaiah, G (1982) : "Poverty in Karnataka : A Socio-Economic Profile", *Margin*, (A quarterly Journal of the NCAER), Delhi.

————————, (1988) : "Concurrent Evaluation of IRDP", *EPW*, February 13.

Thingalaya, N K (1976) : "Marginal Farmers and Agricultural Labourers" *Unpublished Research Report*, Syndicate Bank, Manipal.

Thippaiah, P and M Devendra Babu (1986) : "Tackling Rural Poverty", *Yojana*, Vol.30, No.22, December 1-15.

Tilak, Jandhyala B G (1989) : "Education and Its Relation to Economic Growth, Poverty and Income Distribution : Past Evidence and Further Analysis", 46 World Bank Discussion Paper, The World Bank, Washington. D.C., p.90.

Tilly, L A "Food Entitlement, Famine and Conflict", in Roberg, R I and T K Rabb (ed.) *Hunger and History*, Cambridge, 1985.

Townsend, Peter (ed.) (1970) : *The Concept of Poverty*, Heinemann, London.

Tripathy, R N et.al. (1983) : "Benefits to the Rural Poor : Processes and Prolems of SFDA/IRDP - a Study in Puri District, Orissa", *Journal of Rural Development*, Vol.2, pp.423-43.

UNDP, Human Development Report, *Annual Report*, 1991.

Uphoff, Norman (1986) : *Local Institutional Development*, Kumarian, West Hewford, Connecticut. pp.350-1.

————————, (1986) : *Local Institutional Development : An Analytical Source Book with Cases*, Kumarian Press, P.6.

Usha, B (1984) : "IRDP : The Promise and Performance", *Industrial Economist*, June 15-30.

Vaidyanathan A (1974) : "Some Aspects of Inequalities in Living Standards in Rural India", *Sankhya*, Vol.36, Part c, Parts 2 and 4.

Vanghan, M (1987) : *The Study of an African Famine*, Cambridge.

Venkataramanan, L S et.al. (1985) : Dynamics of Rural Transformation in Karnataka 1956-76, *Research Report*, Institute for Social and Economic Change, Bangalore.

Warnock, John W (1987) : *The Politics of Hunger, The Global Food System*, Methnew, London.

World Bank (1987) : *World Development Report*, Washington DC.

——————, (1992) : Development and Environment, *World Development Report 1992*, Oxford University Press, New York, 1992, p.25.

World Bank Study 1990, "Indonesia : Strategy for a Sustained Reduction in Poverty (Summary and Conclusion) : appeared in *Washington Economic Watch : A Digest of Development Policy Information*, Asia Quarter 1, 1991.

Wright, Robert E (1992) : "A Feminisation of Poverty in Great Britain?", Review of Income and Wealth, Series 38, No.1, March.

Yunus, Muhammad (1988) : *Grameen Bank : Organistion and Operations*, Grameen Bank, Dhaka, Bangladesh, June.

Index